BLACKJACK
for the
CLUELESS

BLACKJACK
for the
CLUELESS

A BEGINNER'S GUIDE TO PLAYING AND WINNING

Walter Thomason

LYLE STUART
Kensington Publishing Corp.
www.kensingtonbooks.com

LYLE STUART books are published by

Kensington Publishing Corp.
850 Third Avenue
New York, NY 10022

Previously published as *The Ultimate Blackjack Book: Basic Strategies, Money Management, and More*. The last three chapters have been previously published in *The Experts' Guide to Casino Games: Expert Gamblers Offer Their Winning Formulas*.

All Kensington titles, imprints, and distributed lines are available at special quantity discounts for bulk purchases for sales promotions, premiums, fund raising, educational, or institutional use. Special book excerpts or customized printings can also be created to fit specific needs. For details, write or phone the office of the Kensington special sales manager: Kensington Publishing Corp., 850 Third Avenue, New York, NY 10022, attn: Special Sales Department, phone 1-800-221-2647.

Kensington and the K logo Reg. U.S. Patent and Trademark Office
Lyle Stuart is a trademark of Kensington Publishing Corp.

First printing 1998

10 9 8 7 6 5 4 3 2

Printed in the United States of America

Library of Congress Cataloging-in-Publication Data

Thomason, Walter.
    Blackjack for the clueless : a beginner's guide to playing and winning / Walter Thomason.
       p.   cm.
    "A Lyle Stuart book."
    Includes bibliographical references (p.).
    ISBN 0-8184-0596-1 (pbk.)
    1. Blackjack (Game) I. Title.
GV1295.B55T476 1998
795.4'23—dc21   98-28474
                                  CIP

CONTENTS

PREFACE

I love blackjack; I love to talk about it, read about it, write about it, and play it! I love the atmosphere of the casinos where the game is dealt, and I love the free or inexpensive entertainment and facilities provided by these casinos. I love the financial risk associated with the game, and the very profitable results that it occasionally provides me.

I also enjoy golfing, fishing, basketball, and the game of chess, and I like an occasional round at the craps table or a visit to the race track, but I *love* blackjack.

My thirty-year fascination with this game, and my continuing observation of how other people play it, prompted me to write this book. I am constantly amazed at how *poorly* most others play blackjack. The majority of players don't fully understand the rules and have no concept of strategy or money management, not to mention card counting or playing tactics, and the casinos do next to nothing to improve the players' chances of winning.

This book is designed for and dedicated to these players. If you are a novice player at blackjack, read this publication and you will become a much better player. If you consider yourself a knowledgeable player, read this book and you will sharpen your skills and improve your chances of winning. If you are an expert at the game, read this book and you will gain insights to the game that you never before considered. Every level of player *will improve* his knowledge and potential by reading this book.

Enjoy your reading, and good luck at the tables!

Walter Thomason

INTRODUCTION

This book contains *everything* that you need to know about the game of blackjack—rules, strategies, playing tactics, money management, card counting, casino conduct, travel tips, casino locations, and more!

One unique aspect of this publication is that it clearly differentiates between *opinion* and *fact* by changing the style of printing. For example, the statement "a standard deck of playing cards (excluding jokers) contains fifty-two cards" is an *indisputable fact*, and is printed in this standard manner.

◆ The statement, "The player should leave the table after losing four consecutive hands" is an *opinion*, and is printed in this type with a small black diamond at the beginning of the paragraph.

In cases where the *overwhelming* opinion is in favor of the statement, it is still treated as an opinion, because everything written about game strategy is based on long-term play.

For many years, writers have attempted to describe the game of 21 as either a mathematical science or as an intellectual art form, when in fact it is more likely a combination of both philosophies—mathematics, statistics, intuition, experience, and luck.

You will notice that the previous sentence was typed in the "opinion" typeface. Get the idea? The reason for this distinction is easily explained by some of the following statements written about his game over the last thirty years by authors who claim to be experts at the game. No names or book titles are used to protect me from lawsuits! These statements are direct quotations from books and magazines about gambling that are currently being sold in bookstores, and although their authors presented them as factual information about the game of blackjack, they are, in reality, opinions.

◆ "Almost all the errors made by a player seem to work to the advantage of the house."

"I have tried to teach several women to become count players; it just doesn't seem to be their bag...they just will not believe that there is an exact way to play a hand."

"You must never play with more than two other players at the table."

"The number of players at the table is immaterial."

"Be sure and always tip the dealer."

"Only tip a dealer if he is helping you win."

"Blackjack games are easy to beat. Once a person has trained himself in the use of a proper system and is adroit with it he will win nine times out of ten."

"In the modern game of blackjack, the player can gain a consistent advantage over the house by using the strategy that is presented in this book."

"There are no miracle systems that give the player a significant advantage over the house."

"Today's casinos, as a whole, are completely honest."

"There was cheating [by the dealers in Las Vegas and Reno] at large, plush casinos...at all betting levels, even for 25 cents!"

"The essential goal behind money management is to bet more when you're winning and less when you're losing...and is virtually impossible to attain."

"If you win 50 percent [of your original bankroll] in one session, quit playing."

"Keep winning as long as you can."

Obviously, these statements represent the *opinion* of the authors, and may have little or no basis in fact. Consequently, typeface changes will be used throughout this book to identify *fact* from opinion, conjecture, anecdotal stories, personal preferences, misinformation, and pure fantasy!

I recommend that you read this book from start to finish, since gaining expertise at this game is a step-by-step process, beginning with an understanding of the basic rules and ending with an overall philosophy of play that will greatly improve your chances of winning.

For casual reading, when you're not in the mood to concentrate, turn to the concluding chapter entitled "Potpourri." This chapter contains odds and ends that are interesting and informative, and could have a profound effect on how you implement your playing skills.

I appreciate your purchase of this book, and welcome your reactions regarding its contents. Please send your opinions or queries to the publisher, and ask that they be forwarded to me.

ACKNOWLEDGMENTS

My thanks to my wife, Cynthia, for her editorial support, and to my gambling buddies, John Loudis and Bob Henninger, for reviewing the initial drafts of this book.

Thanks also to Donald Currier, Editor of *Las Vegas Insider*, for his insightful critique of the final draft.

And thanks to my mom for teaching me the basics of the game when I was a teenager. It took me years to figure out why she always wanted to be the dealer!

My special gratitude to the unknown individual who first created the game of blackjack. His invention has been a source of personal consternation and fascination for many, many years!

BLACKJACK
for the
CLUELESS

History of Gambling
and Blackjack

"The world's second oldest diversion."

—ESQUIRE

*"It is the child of avarice, the brother of iniquity, and
the father of mischief."*

—GEORGE WASHINGTON

◆   Man, by nature, instinct, DNA, or whatever, is a *gambler.*
Homo sapiens, along with having a prehensile thumb and a larger
brain than the competition, was one of the few species willing to
take a chance. Archeologists have identified many prehistoric
creatures who became extinct due to their inability to risk
change, move into the unknown, or defy the odds.

Ancient history presents many examples of human civilizations
that failed when they became inflexible to taking risks, and were
overwhelmed by other groups who retained the capacity to
gamble on their future. Complacency seems to lead to stagnation,
and the capacity to take a chance, to *gamble,* has often led to the
advancement of our civilization.

Adam and Eve are portrayed as being the first gamblers when they chose to eat the forbidden fruit in the Garden of Eden, and their descendants have carried on this tradition. Do you think that prehistoric man was taking a chance—gambling—when he decided to attack a Mastodon?

It's logical to assume that if our species gambled for its existence, it would also invent ways to gamble for pleasure.

In fact, the word *gamble* originates from the Middle English (ca. 1150–1475) word *gamenen*, meaning "to play." There is no historical period or culture known where gambling for pleasure was not present. Dice, carved from animal bones and natural materials, seem to have been the choice among ancient Greek and Judaic cultures, and the Egyptians favored a game called *Atep*, played by guessing the number of fingers held up by an opponent.

The Romans preferred wagering on gladiatorial fights and chariot races. Betting on horse races became popular among monarchs during the Middle Ages, and England's famous King John kept special racing horses in his stables.

Playing cards first appeared in Asia shortly after the Chinese invented paper in the first century A.D. and decks of cards were popular in fourteenth-century Italy and France. Playing cards accompanied Columbus to the New World on his first voyage.

European visitors to the Western Hemisphere soon discovered that Native Americans participated in many games of chance, including wagering on dice games, an early version of football, horse races, and other athletic contests.

Lotteries were popular in England and in the Colonies, and the Revolutionary War was financed in part by a lottery established by the Continental Congress.

Riverboat gambling began in the 1800s, while gaming houses were popular in San Francisco, Colorado Springs, and Denver during the Gold Rush and silver strike period in the West.

The history of the game of blackjack is somewhat obscure. The forerunner to the standard deck of blackjack cards, the same as any fifty-two card deck, first appeared in China and India, and became popular in Europe in the fourteenth century. The French created the modern deck of cards, based on Tarot cards, consisting of fifty-two cards and four suits.

Blackjack was the generic casino game (also known as Vingt-et-un, Pontoon, VanJohn, Einund-Zwanzig, Achtzehn-und-Drie, or Twenty one), and its inventor is unknown.

The popularity of gambling has ebbed and flowed throughout the history of the United States. Consumer complaints over illegal and fraudulent practices have caused governmental agencies to ban all types of gaming at one time or another. For instance, Nevada closed its casinos in 1910, and did not resume legal gaming until the 1930s.

Mafia money led to the return of casino gambling in Nevada, and eventually state regulatory agencies gained control over the honesty of the games and the integrity of those financing the casinos.

The possibility of encountering fraudulent or dishonest gaming in this state is almost nonexistent at this time.

Edward Thorp changed the public attitude about casino gambling and blackjack when he wrote his 1962 book, *Beat the Dealer*, which gave players a statistically proven method of winning. The growth in the number of gamblers, ready to reap the benefits of Thorp's book, soon led to a major increase in clientele in Nevada. Casino owners quickly realized that more players equaled more profits, since most of the newcomers failed to apply the proper playing strategies recommended in Thorp's book.

After his second edition was released, using Julian Braun's improvements in computer analysis, blackjack became as popular as craps in most Las Vegas casinos.

Legalized casino gambling went national in 1978, when Resorts International opened in Atlantic City. Within two months, gross profits from table games alone were in the $200,000 per day range, and at present there are eleven major casino resorts (with more under construction) in this New Jersey coastal city.

Riverboat and tribal casinos have provided the most recent geographic expansion in this industry. On April Fool's Day, 1991, riverboat gambling began in Iowa. Within the next two years, state governments in Illinois, Mississippi, Louisiana, Missouri, and Indiana approved casino gaming on "water-based" facilities, and agreed to regulate these enterprises for a share of the profits.

The federal government opened the doors for legalized casinos on Indian reservations in 1988, with the enactment of the Indian Gaming Regulatory Act (Public Law 100-497), leading to the establishment of casinos in many states where casino games are still disallowed. The growth and development of tribal casino gaming is explained in the "Potpourri" chapter of this book.

Casino cruise ships have also gained popularity over the last ten years, especially in Florida. These ships operate outside of territorial waters, offering short "cruises to nowhere," thus avoiding taxing and regulatory restrictions. Major cruise lines have also expanded their casinos to accommodate their gaming oriented vacationers.

The casino gaming industry is currently in a state of continuous growth, development, and adjustment, as this multi-billion dollar industry attempts to market its product to the growing numbers of people who enjoy the recreational and potentially profitable benefits of this activity.

The knowledgeable gambler is the one who seeks out those establishments that offer the *best playing opportunities*, and takes advantage of the many "perks" offered in this competitive marketing atmosphere.

Gambling in this country is reaching its greatest popularity at the present time. Indian gaming, riverboats, and gambling ships now compete with land-based casinos, horse and dog tracks, jai-alai palaces, bingo halls, lotteries, and poker rooms to the extent that as of 1994, forty-eight states and ten Canadian provinces now permit some form of legalized gambling. Governmental units need additional revenues, and are often willing to oversee the honesty and integrity of legalized gambling in order to receive a share of the profits.

◆   Knowing the preceding information can be quite useful to you while you are sitting at a table waiting for the dealer to shuffle a six-deck shoe. It's sometimes fun to turn to the player sitting next to you and say, "Did you know that..."

Also, if anyone should ever ask you *why* you like to gamble, you can say, "It's part of my ancestral heritage!" and then provide them with some of the preceding historical information.

Basic Rules of Play

*"Always do right; this will gratify some people
and astonish the rest."*

—Mark Twain

Rules of the Game

Blackjack is a fairly simple game to play. The object is to make a wager in advance that you, the player, will draw a combination of cards equal to or less than 21 points in value, and that your total score will be closer to 21 points than the dealer—your only opponent.

The cards dealt to you and the dealer are those contained in any standard deck of playing cards, often referred to as a "poker deck." They contain four cards each of thirteen values (2, 3, 4, 5, 6, 7, 8, 9, 10, jack, queen, king, and ace). To determine the number of points in your hand, the following applies:

1. All numerical cards count their face value (a 5 of diamonds is five points).

2. The jack, queen, and king each count as ten points.

3. The ace counts as one or eleven points, depending on your preference (more on this later).

The person (dealer or player) who has the higher total number of points without exceeding a point count of twenty-one wins the wager. If the player and the dealer have identical point counts at the conclusion of the hand of play, the hand is a *push*, or tie, and no money changes hands.

If the player *exceeds* a point count of twenty-one, he automatically loses, regardless of what the dealer does later in the hand.

If the dealer *exceeds* a point count of twenty-one, he pays all players who still remain in the game (those with a point count of 21 or less).

A *blackjack* (also called a *natural*) is any ten-point card and an ace received by the dealer or player in the first two cards dealt. If the player has a blackjack, and the dealer does not, the dealer pays the player one and one-half times the amount originally wagered.

If the dealer has a blackjack, and the player doesn't, the dealer wins the amount of the original wager.

If the player and the dealer both have blackjack (a ten-point card and an ace), the hand is a *push*, and no money is exchanged.

The suits of the cards (hearts, spades, diamonds, clubs) play *no part* in the play of the basic game.

You, as a player, are only playing and wagering against the dealer. The actions of the other players that may be seated at the table (up to six players in most casinos), have no affect on your wager with the dealer. It's possible for you to win a hand against the dealer while every other player loses to him; it's also possible to lose while every other player wins.

The Blackjack Table

Blackjack tables are essentially the same in every casino. The table top is one-half of a circle, with an area for the dealer to stand on the flat side, and six spaces for players to sit and play around the semicircle.

Each player faces the dealer, and has a betting box or circle imprinted on the table in front of his seat. Wagers are placed in the betting box by each player prior to the dealing of the cards, telling the dealer which players wish to play the next hand. Generally, a player may sit down at a table and place a bet at any time, even if cards are being dealt to other players, and will be automatically dealt a hand on the next round of play. Some casinos have tables which disallow "mid-shoe entry," meaning that new players are not allowed to enter the game after the first card is dealt from the deck or "shoe" (a shoe is a box that holds cards in a multiple deck game), and the dealer will inform you that you cannot play until the deck(s) has been dealt and the cards have been reshuffled.

The surface of the table provides important information to potential players, and should be read and considered prior to play. The information normally provided, without the necessity of asking the dealer, is as follows:

1. *Blackjack pays 3 to 2.* This informs the player that an ace and a ten-point card is an automatic winner of one and one-half times the amount originally wagered, if the dealer doesn't also have a blackjack.

2. *Dealer must hit on 16, and stand on 17.* This rule tells the player that the dealer *must* draw cards until his hand exceeds sixteen points, and that he can draw no further cards if his hand totals seventeen points or more, regardless of the players' cards. Once the dealer has seventeen points, he must stand.

3. *Insurance pays 2 to 1.* An insurance bet is an additional wager that you can make if the dealer has a ace as his exposed card. This wager, which is normally the amount of the original wager, insures that the dealer does not win the original bet if he has a blackjack.

4. *Table minimum and maximum bet.* The least and the most that you can bet at a table is normally displayed on a standing placard to the left of the dealer. A typical placard might read as follows:

Minimum Bet $5, Maximum Bet $200. This tells the player that he may wager from $5 to $200 as an initial bet.

5. *"Exotic Rules."* There are many new variations in wagering, which involve combinations of cards that pay big bonuses if they occur and if the player has made a separate wager in anticipation of their occurrence, such as being dealt two or three 7s in a row, or two cards of the same suit in a row, etc. The rules for these wagers and the potential win ratios are normally displayed on a separate placard to the right of the dealer, or in some other conspicuous area on or above the table. The basic game of blackjack is unaffected by these additional variations; the same basic rules apply, and betting on combinations of cards is not required.

Taking a minute to examine a blackjack table prior to placing a wager may save you the embarrassment of being told that you are ineligible to play.

Playing the Game

At this point in your reading, you have learned the basic rules of the game. You know how to "read" a table, and are ready to sit down, place a bet, and play the game.

Much like the rules and the table design, the game is played in the same fashion in almost every casino.

At the initiation of play, or whenever the cards are being replaced with new cards, the dealer spreads the deck(s) across the table, face up, to be sure that they contain the correct number of cards in each deck and that none of the cards are flawed in any manner. Assuming the cards are undamaged and the count is correct, the dealer shuffles the cards, requests that a player "cut" the deck with a separate plastic cut card, and begins the game.

Players are asked to place their wagers if they have not yet done so, and chips are exchanged for cash for those wishing to bet. Playing chips are required in most casinos and may be purchased from a cashier or from the dealer prior to play. You will notice that all cash that crosses the table in exchange for chips is verified by at least two casino employees. This policy insures that you receive the correct amount of chips in exchange for your cash, and prevents any nefarious conduct between the player and the dealer.

Casinos are extremely concerned about the honesty and integrity of their employees and customers, and go to great lengths to insure that they are not cheated. The use of actual cash on the table is discouraged by most casinos, but might be permitted in some situations if the player requests that his "cash play." The dealer will normally stop the game and call his supervisor, the pit boss, to approve this request.

The dealing of cards to players who have placed bets varies to some degree, depending on the number of decks being used in the game, but the pattern of dealing the cards is universal. The dealer always discards the first card in the deck or shoe, then deals from his left to his right, each player in rotation receiving one card, and the dealer receiving one card, face up. The players then receive a second card in rotation, and the dealer gives himself a second card, face down. There is a major difference as to how players receive their cards, depending on how many decks are being used. The differences in play are as follows:

A. If the dealer is using only *one or two* decks of cards, the cards dealt to the players are normally dealt *face down*, and the players may pick up their cards and examine them to determine their playing decisions. The dealer holds the deck(s) in his hand throughout the game.

B. If the dealer is using *multiple decks* (normally four to eight decks), the shuffled decks are contained in a plastic or wooden box called a "shoe," and all cards to players are dealt *face up. Players are not allowed to touch the cards at any time.*

Most casinos currently use a shoe and six decks, but one- and two-deck games are still offered in many establishments.

Whatever the case, the dealer always has one concealed card and one exposed card, and the player has two cards, either face up or concealed, on the first round of the deal.

On those occasions when the dealer has an ace as his exposed card, he will ask all players if they wish to take "insurance," prior to continuing the deal. This bet pays "2 to 1" *if* the dealer has a blackjack. If not, the bet is lost and removed from the table.

The player who has an ace and a ten-point card, a "natural," may elect to take "even money," an immediate payoff on his original bet (not the normal 3 to 2 payoff on a blackjack) by requesting insurance and asking for "even money" when the dealer has an ace exposed. In effect, an insurance bet allows the player to win one wager at 2 to 1 odds and lose his original bet if the dealer has blackjack. If the dealer doesn't have blackjack, the player loses the insurance bet and must still beat the dealer's final hand to win the original bet.

Once the possibility of insurance bets is resolved, the dealer initiates the second and most crucial round of play. Players are *required* to make at least one of four possible decisions: stand, hit, split, or double-down. Each player must also inform the dealer of his choice of action, either verbally or by hand motion. An explanation of each possible decision, and the action that must be taken by the player, is described below. At the moment, you are learning *what* to do; *why* you make a particular decision is explained in subsequent chapters of this book.

Stand   The simplest decision to make is to *stand*, which tells the dealer that you wish to add no further cards to your hand. Due to the high noise level in most casinos, and in order to avoid any misunderstanding as to your choice of action, various hand signals are used to tell the dealer what you wish to do.

In multiple-deck games employing a shoe, simply wave one hand, palm down, over your two exposed cards if you wish to stand. Remember that the dealer rotates around the table from left to right, so you must wait your turn.

In single- or double-deck games, where the dealer has dealt your initial two cards face down, simply slide your cards *under* your wager if you wish to stand. *Do not touch your wager with your hands at any time.* Casino personnel are always on the lookout for players who might attempt to alter their wager after seeing their cards, so never touch your initial bet until after the hand is over and you have been paid by the dealer.

Verbally, you simply say to the dealer, "Stand."

You *must* stand on *every* hand dealt to you, even if you previously employ one of the other three options available to you (hit, split, double-down). This will be explained as the other options are discussed. Note: It is *impossible to "bust" your hand* (exceed a point count of twenty-one) if you stand on your first two cards. You continue to be a player in the hand until the dealer either ties or beats your point count. If the dealer exceeds a point count of twenty-one, you are a winner, regardless of the number of points in your hand.

Hit Hit is a request to the dealer that you wish to add one or more cards to the original two cards that were dealt to you. The hand motions to receive additional cards are as follows:

In multiple-deck games, where your initial two cards are dealt face-up, place your hand, palm down, near your cards, cup your hand slightly, and scrape your fingers across the table toward you. This "beckoning" motion tells the dealer that you want a hit. Repeat the action if you wish additional cards. When you decide you want no additional cards added to your hand, revert to the "Stand" motion previously explained, and the dealer will proceed to the next player.

In single- or double-deck games, hold your two cards in your hand

and brush them across the table toward you if you wish a hit. When you wish to stand, slide your cards under your wager.

In any game the verbal request for additional cards is, "hit," or "hit me."

If your point count exceeds twenty-one points at any time after taking one or more hits, you automatically lose the hand, and the dealer removes your cards and places your lost wager in the chip tray in front of him. You are no longer considered to be a player in the hand, even if the dealer later exceeds twenty-one points and busts his hand.

Split   Most casinos offer the player the option of separating the first two cards dealt *if they are a pair (two 3s, two 7s),* thus creating two separate hands. A wager equal to the original amount bet must be placed on the table, normally beside the initial wager. In multiple-deck games, the dealer will verify your intention to split the hand and separate the two cards, placing one wager behind each hand. He will then deal to the hand to his left, which must be completed before cards are dealt to the other new hand. Stand, hit, split, and double-down rules normally apply to each new hand being dealt. Again, if either hand exceeds twenty-one points it is an automatic loser. In single- or double-deck games, the player places the original two cards *face up* on the table, and matches the original wager. The dealer verifies the player's intention to split, and deals to each hand as in the multiple-deck game.

Casino rules vary on how many times a player may split his cards. For instance, if you draw a pair of eights, split them, and draw another eight, most casinos will allow you to split again and start a third hand. When a pair of aces are drawn, you are normally allowed only *one* card on each hand. Ask about split rules before you begin play.

Double-Down   The fourth option available to you is that of doubling down, which allows you the option of doubling your original wager and receiving one, *and only one*, hit card. Most casinos allow a player to double-down when the player has an original point count of nine, ten, or eleven, and many allow doubling-down on any first two cards. Check with the dealer if rules are not posted on the information placard on the table.

In multiple-deck games, a player may double-down by placing a bet equal to his original bet. The dealer will verify that you wish to double-down, and deal one card, *face up and turned sideways*, to indicate to his supervisor that you chose to double-down. He then proceeds to the next player.

In single-deck games, you lay both cards on the table, *face up, and place a bet equal to your original bet*. The dealer will deal you one card, usually face down, and proceed to the next player. In some casinos the player may be allowed to "double-down for less," or play the one-card draw option while increasing the amount of the original wager by less than an equal amount. If your bankroll is a problem, you can always ask the dealer if this is allowed.

Concluding the Hand

After every player has completed playing his hand (by standing, hitting, splitting, or doubling-down), the dealer plays out his hand in the following manner:

1. He first turns over his hole card and exposes it to the players. Most casinos require that the dealer must hit his hand, and continue hitting his hand, if his initial point count is sixteen or less, and he must stand if his point count is seventeen or more, regardless of the point count of the hands held by the players. These rules are normally printed across the surface of the blackjack table.

2. If the dealer's point count exceeds twenty-one points, his hand is a "bust," and he pays all remaining players an amount equal to their wagers.

3. If his point count does not exceed twenty-one points, he compares his hand with those of the players remaining in the game. Starting from right to left, he either:

A. Collects the player's bet if his point count is higher than that of the player.

B. Pays the player an amount equal to his wager if the player's point count is higher than that of the dealer.

C. Taps or pats the table in front of those players who have a point count equal to that of the dealer, indicating that the hand is a "push," or tie, and that no money changes hands.

After collecting or paying all wagers, the dealer removes all used cards from the table and places them in a discard stack or container. He removes the cards from the table *in such a way that the hands can be reconstructed if there is any dispute regarding the outcome of play.*

As each hand is concluded, players may remove their winnings from the table as well as their original wagers, and may then place any new wager as allowed by the minimum and maximum table limits. Cards are dealt to players who have placed bets, and the process is repeated until the designated end of the deck or shoe. Once the "cut" card is reached, the dealer completes the hand currently in play, and then reshuffles the cards.

Other Important Aspects of the Game

- The dealer has no opportunity to split or double-down; this is a player's option only.
- A player may never remove a wager, or touch his wager, during the playing of a hand.
- A player may withdraw from play and leave the table at the completion of any hand.
- A player may ask to be "passed over" for the play of one or more hands. Casino rules vary, but most allow players to skip a hand or two in the middle of a deck or shoe.

- A player may play more than one hand at a time if additional positions are available at the table. Some casinos require that the player wager at least twice the table minimum if he chooses to play more than one hand.

Blackjack Variations

Occasionally, new ways of playing the game are introduced. Two of the newest and most popular variations are Triple Action blackjack and Double Exposure blackjack.

In Triple Action blackjack, the player makes three separate wagers on his initial hand. The dealer plays against the hand and the first wager, and then replaces his hole card with a new card for each of the player's next two wagers. The outcome of the second and third wager is based on dealer's new hole card. The player may win or lose one or more of the bets, but automatically loses all wagers if he busts the hand. The dealer can win, lose, or push on each hand, depending on the results of play on each new hole card that he receives.

In Double Exposure blackjack, *all* cards, including the dealer's hole card, are dealt face up. Several rule changes offset the fact that the dealer's hole card is exposed (blackjack pays even money, ties go to the dealer, etc.).

A complete explanation of these hybrid games is beyond the scope of this book, but a few words of advice may improve your chances of winning at them.

◆ When playing Triple Action blackjack, play as if you were playing regular blackjack. The tendency is to not apply basic strategy rules for fear of busting the hand and immediately losing all three wagers. As a later chapter of this book will tell you, basic strategy must be followed if you hope to be a long-term winner.

Incidentally, expert card counters (explained in a later chapter) claim that they can profit from this game because wagers can be increased without attracting undue attention from casino personnel.

In regard to Double Exposure blackjack, I advise that you *not* play this game. The advantages to the house created by rule changes far exceed the benefits of knowing the value of the dealer's hole card.

The rules described in this chapter are those practiced by almost every legal gambling establishment in this country. In general, the more liberal the rules, the more beneficial to the knowledgeable blackjack player.

Variations to the game occur frequently, based on player demand and casino innovation, so it is always wise to check out the rules prior to playing in any casino.

◆   It amazes me that many people who play this game, perhaps as many as twenty percent of those who risk their money in hopes of winning, *don't understand the basic rules of the game!* Like sacrificial lambs, they cast their cash on the table, tell every person around them that they don't really know how to play, try to get twenty-one points on every hand, and laugh when they lose! It's enough to make me want to open my own casino!

Each chapter of this book that offers instructional information is followed by a short multiple-choice quiz to test your comprehension. Take the time to answer the questions, and be sure that you score 100 percent on each quiz. Blackjack, in the long run, offers a very small percentage advantage to the best of players; be sure that you fully understand the basics of play if you want to be a consistent winner.

Answer the questions on the following pages to test your knowledge of the basic rules.

Basic Rules Quiz

The following quiz is designed to test your knowledge of the basic rules of blackjack. If you don't answer all of the questions correctly, reread this chapter!! Don't attempt to play in a casino until you know the basics. I estimate that at least 20 percent of those who sit down to play do not know the rules of the game, much to the delight of casino owners.

Quiz 1–Basic Rules

1. What is the point value of an ace?
   a. One point.
   b. Eleven points.
   c. One or eleven points.
   d. All of the above.

2. What happens if the dealer and the player both have a "natural"?
   a. The player wins his original wager.
   b. The dealer wins the wager.
   c. The player wins one and one-half times his original wager.
   d. The hand is a draw, or "push."

3. Who is your opponent in blackjack?
   a. The other players.
   b. The dealer.
   c. The player with the best hand.
   d. The pit boss.

4. Most casinos stipulate that:
   a. The dealer must hit on 16 and stand on 17.
   b. A blackjack pays 2 to 3.

    c. Insurance pays even money.

    d. The player can only play one hand at a time.

5. The object of the game is to:
   a. Win money.
   b. Draw cards until you have twenty-one points.
   c. Beat the other players at the table.
   d. All of the above.

6. Most casinos require that you:
   a. Play with cash only.
   b. Play with chips only.
   c. Purchase chips at the cashier's cage.
   d. Establish a credit line before playing.

7. What happens before the dealer initiates play at a table?
   a. The dealer shuffles the cards.
   b. A player cuts the cards.
   c. All wagers are placed in the betting boxes before any cards are dealt.
   d. All of the above.

8. What are the decisions that the player must make during the play of *every* hand?
   a. Stand.
   b. Hit.
   c. Split (if paired).
   d. Double-down.
   e. All of the above.
   f. None of the above.

9. What is a "split"?
   a. The player splits his bet between two separate hands.

    b. The player splits a pair, matches his original bet, and plays two separate hands.

    c. The dealer splits the deck and deals from the left hand stack of cards.

    d. The player forms a partnership with another player and splits profits or losses.

10. Who wins if the dealer exceeds a point count of twenty-one?

    a. All players who initially placed a wager.

    b. All players who have a point count of twenty-one or less.

    c. Any player who drew less than three cards.

    d. All of the above.

    e. None of the above.

11. What happens if chips are left in the betting box at the conclusion of a hand?

    a. The dealer asks the player to remove the chips and place a new wager for the next hand.

    b. The chips become the wager for the next hand.

    c. The chips are considered to be a tip for the dealer.

    d. The chips become the property of the casino if not removed before the next deal.

12. What advantage(s) does the player have over the dealer?

    a. The dealer can't split or double-down.

    b. The dealer can only play one hand.

    c. The dealer must hit on 16 or under.

    d. The dealer must stand on 17 or over.

    e. The player can quit playing after any hand; the dealer must deal down to the cut card.

    f. The player is paid 3 to 2 on blackjack; the dealer only gets the player's initial bet.

g. The player can leave the table with his profits; the dealer must continue playing, regardless of wins or losses.

h. The player can wager any amount between the minimum and maximum allowed at the table; the dealer can only collect or pay the amount wagered by the player.

i. The player can only lose what he wagers; the dealer must pay all winning wagers, regardless of the loss to the casino.

j. The player can alter his playing decisions based on his knowledge of the game and the flow of the cards; the dealer must follow pre-established rules, regardless of the player's cards.

k. All of the above.

Answers to Basic Rules Quiz:

1. c   2. d   3. b   4. a   5. a   6. b   7. d   8. e   9. b   10. b.
11. b   12. k

Basic Strategy

*"I don't think we can win every game.
Just the next one."*

—LOU HOLTZ

The basic rules of blackjack explain the mechanical aspects of playing the game; *Basic Strategy tells you the playing decisions that you should make to improve your chances of winning.*

Your decision to either stand, hit, split, or double-down is crucial to being successful at this game, and Basic Strategy tells you the mathematically correct decision to make.

The word "strategy" also implies a long-term program to achieve an overall goal—in this case to make money playing this game by following a predetermined plan over a long period of time. This distinction is important, since all basic strategy decisions are based on *millions of hands of play*, and may or may not be beneficial in the short run.

Prior to the 1960s, there was no mathematically proven method to tell the player which playing decisions he should make—when to stand, hit, split, or double-down. Players were required to make decisions based on intuition, instinct, luck, or recommendations from friends or self-appointed experts. Many unskilled players still use these archaic methods when they play, much to the delight of casino owners.

The computer, and a few writers knowledgeable enough to use its capabilities, totally altered the nature of how the game is dealt and played, and led to its incredible growth in popularity.

Edward Thorp, then a college professor, studied previous research conducted by computer expert Julian Braun and others, spent time at the blackjack tables in Las Vegas, and wrote the aforementioned book entitled *Beat the Dealer: A Winning Strategy for the Game of 21*. It gained national attention and became a best seller.

This work was unique because it told the player when to stand, hit, split, or double-down on the mathematical probability of improving the hand or beating the dealer. In essence, the book taught the average player how to reduce the house advantage to an almost even-money proposition, based on the *long-term* probabilities of winning or losing.

Many other writers followed up with additional studies of basic strategy, and all of their works are based on computer simulated play, with minor variations based on casino rule changes. The important fact to remember is that *nearly all basic strategy rules are indisputable in the long run;* the finite nature of mathematical science dictates that a particular playing decision, based on the player's cards and the dealer's exposed card, will yield a predictable outcome after millions of hands of play.

For example, if a player has a point count of eleven on his first two cards, and the dealer has a six as his exposed card, the player will win the hand more often than he loses the hand if the proper strategy recommendation is followed. Likewise, if the player has a point count of sixteen on the first two cards, the dealer will win more often than the player, regardless of the dealer's up-card!

Basic strategy tells the player what action he should take, *for each and every possible card combination*, and tells him his probable chance of winning or losing each particular hand.

Basic Strategy Rules

◆   The rules of basic strategy require that you apply these two basic principles:

1. *Always* follow them.
2. *Never* vary from them.

These principles are overstated because the average player is much like the average human being, who often believes that "rules don't apply in this case," "rules are made to be broken," "rules are for players who don't understand the game like I do," etc.

Basic strategy rules should never be broken, at any time, regardless of playing conditions, size of wager, amount won or lost, or personal disposition. Basic strategy rules should be obeyed if you wish to play blackjack in a way that gives you the most *mathematically probable* chance of winning. Even if the player is an expert card counter he doesn't *ignore* basic strategy; he *alters* it to allow for the current count.

In truth, the advent of basic strategy has taken much of the adventure out of playing the game, and if properly followed has practically eliminated *personal decision-making on the part of the player.* There are few choices to make; simply follow the recommended rules of play and hope for the best!

It's my opinion that most players don't choose to give up the option of personal decision-making, and continue to provide money for the expansion and improvement of gambling casinos.

As strange as it may seem, several prominent writers of blackjack books advise players to *ignore* the odds proven by computer simulation, and follow a basic strategy program based on the writer's personal preferences! These variations in computer-generated recommendations generally require that the player be more aggressive when the dealer shows a weak hand, and be more conservative when the dealer shows a strong hand.

For instance, some writers tell the player to double-down with a hard count of eight when the dealer shows a six, or *not* to split aces when the dealer shows a nine through ace. I personally disagree with these variations from computer analyzed basic strategy, and recommend playing by the odds established by long-term statistical analysis—not by recommendations based on the personal opinion of a writer.

Another premise of basic strategy is that it is based on the long-run nature of the cards being dealt. *Almost anything is possible in the short run;* basic strategy only tells you your odds of winning or losing in the long run. The progression of cards from a deck or shoe may greatly vary from long-run expectations.

In other words, it's your money—wager it as you choose, and ignore the outraged comments of the players around you and the surprised expression on the dealer's face. If it's your disposition to take chances beyond the realm of statistical probability, feel free to do so, but keep in mind that the overall odds are always in effect.

In your defense, it's an absolute fact that the actions of an individual player (in this case, your actions if you ignore basic strategy) *have no overall long-term effect on the other players at the table.* Players tend to remember the big hands that they lost when another player didn't follow basic strategy, and forget about the time when they won because of another player's "mistake."

What the Experts Say

◆   My personal knowledge of basic strategy is based on what I've read over the last twenty years. It seems logical to assume that those who write best-selling books about this game should be providing accurate information to their readers.

Since I don't have access to sophisticated computers, and don't have the desire to "reinvent the wheel," I assumed that writers of gambling books would provide accurate and consistent information to readers.

Consequently, I reviewed the basic strategy section of every gambling book that I've purchased in the last five years—thirteen books by different authors, each stating that his recommendations *must* be followed if the player hopes to be a long-term winner.

The summary of this compilation of data is illustrated in the chart below:

Basic Strategy for the Multideck Game
(Double-Down After Split Permitted)
The Dealer's Up-Card

YOUR HAND	2	3	4	5	6	7	8	9	10	A
5	H	H	H	H	H	H	H	H	H	H
6	H	H	H	H	H	H	H	H	H	H
7	H	H	H	H	H	H	H	H	H	H
8	H	H	H	H/D	H/D	H	H	H	H	H
9	H/D	D	D	D	D	D	H	H	H	H
10	D	D	D	D	D	D	D	D	H	H/D
11	D/H	D/H	D/H	D/H	D/H	D/H	D/H	D/H	D/H	H/D
12	H	H	S	S	S	H	H	H	H	H
13	S	S	S	S	S	H	H	H	H	H
14	S	S	S	S	S	H	H	H	H	H
15	S	S	S	S	S	H	H	H	H	H
16	S	S	S	S	S	H	H	H	H	H
17	S	S	S	S	S	S	S	S	S	S
18	S	S	S	S	S	S	S	S	S	S
19	S	S	S	S	S	S	S	S	S	S
A/2	H	H	H/D	D/H	D	H	H	H	H	H
A/3	H	H	H/D	D/H	D	H	H	H	H	H
A/4	H	H	D/H	D/H	D	H	H	H	H	H

YOUR HAND	2	3	4	5	6	7	8	9	10	A
A/5	H	H	D/H	D/H	D	H	H	H	H	H
A/6	H	D/H	D/S	D/S	D	H	H	H	H	H
A/7	S	D/S	D/S	D/S	D/S	S	S	H/S	H/S	H/S
A/8	S	S	S	S	S	S	S	S	S	S
A/9	S	S	S	S	S	S	S	S	S	S
A/A	P	P	P	P	P	P	P	P	P	P
2/2	P/H	P/H	P	P	P	H	H	H	H	H
3/3	P/H	P/H	P	P	P	P	H	H	H	H
4/4	H	H	H	H/P	H/P	H	H	H	H	H
5/5	D	D	D	D	D	D	D	D	H	H/D
6/6	P/H	P/H	P/S	P/S	P/S	H	H	H	H	H
7/7	P	P	P	P	P	P	P/H	H	H	H
8/8	P	P	P	P	P	P	P	P	P	P
9/9	P	P	P	P	P	S	P/S	P/S	S	S
10/10	S	S	S	S	S	S	S	S	S	S

H = Hit   S = Stand   D = Double-Down   P = Split

If square is split, first equals majority opinion and second equals minority opinion.

◆ An explanation of the preceding chart is as follows:

1. The recommended strategy is based on multideck games (four or more decks) that allow the player to double-down after splitting pairs, with only one card allowed after splitting aces.

2. The top horizontal numbers indicate the value of the dealer's exposed card.

3. The left side vertical column of numbers indicate the values of the player's initial two cards.

Starting from the top, the numbers 5 through 17 are *hard count totals* of the first two cards dealt to the player (excluding hands with aces or pairs).

The remaining numbers, A/2 through A/A are *soft hands*, and 2/2 through 10/10 are potential *split hands*.

4. The letters within the squares (H, S, D, or P) stand for Hit, Stand, Double-Down, or Split, and indicate the recommendations of the authors of the thirteen books reviewed.

Where only one letter is in a square, at least twelve of thirteen authors made the same recommendation.

When the square is split by a line, and two letters appear in the same square, the first letter represents the *majority* opinion, (seven to eleven authors) and the second letter represents the *minority* opinion (two to six authors). Squares with two letters indicate that writers of gambling books often disagree as to which basic strategy decision is most advantageous to the player!

5. To read the chart, select the number in the left-hand vertical column that represents the point count in your hand, move across the chart to the square that represents the value of the dealer's exposed card (as illustrated in the top horizontal column), and follow the recommendation contained in the box (Hit, Stand, Double-Down, or Split).

For instance, if your hand is A/4, and the dealer's up-card is 3, the experts recommend that you hit the hand. If your hand is A/7, and the dealer's exposed card is 5, the majority of the experts suggest that you should double-down, while the minority of the experts suggest that you stand.

6. The minority opinions expressed by the authors surveyed often reflect their aggressive or conservative approach to the game. Occasionally the statistical differences are so minute that either suggestion is acceptable.

7. My personal thoughts regarding Basic Strategy are not included in this chart, but will be addressed later in this book.

"No-Brainers"

◆   A review of the preceding chart indicates that there are many situations when only one decision is advisable. A summation of these "no-brainer" hands, and the rationale for each decision, is listed below:

1. Your hard hand totals 5, 6, or 7, against any dealer's up-card. Decision: *Hit*. You can only improve the hand, and have limited your chances of winning by not drawing at least one card.

2. Your hard hand totals 12 through 16, when the dealer's exposed card is 17 or higher. Decision: *Hit*. Your combination of cards, known as "stiff" hands, are the worst cards that a player can receive. The chances of you winning when the dealer has a potentially pat hand are extremely poor, but the chances of hitting the hand and improving it are better than standing with your initial two-card total point count.

3. Your hard hand totals 13 through 16, and the dealer's exposed card is 2 through 6. Decision: *Stand*. The dealer must continue to hit his hand until his point count is 17 or better, and the chances that he will bust are greater than your chances of improving your hand.

4. Your hard hand totals 17, against the dealer's any up-card. Decision: *Stand*. Even though your hand may not be a winner, the chances of improving it don't merit hitting it.

5. Your soft hand is A/2 through A/6, while the dealer's exposed card is 7 or higher. Decision: *Hit, do not double*. Your chances of winning these hands by hitting one or more times are greater than doubling the hands when only one card is allowed.

6. Your soft hand is A/8 or A/9, against the dealer's any up card. Decision: *Stand*. A hand totaling nineteen or twenty points, either soft or hard, is usually a winning hand.

7. Your hand is A/A, against the dealer's any up-card. Decision: *Split*. Although it is possible to either hit, split, or double-down on these two cards, splitting the aces and drawing one card to each offers the best odds of winning or breaking even. The statistical analysis of this situation is complicated but indisputable.

8. Your hand is a pair of 2s, 3s, 4s, or 6s, facing a dealer's 8 or higher. Decision: *Hit*. Even though it is usually legal to split these hands, the statistical odds clearly indicate that hitting rather than splitting against these possible pat hands is advisable.

9. Your hand is a pair of 8s, against the dealer's any up-card. Decision: *Split*. Always splitting 8s may be one of the most difficult decisions that a player must make, especially if the stakes are high and the dealer's exposed card is a 10 or an ace, but almost every expert agrees that splitting the hand, and following up with the appropriate hit, double-down, or resplit, provides the player with the best chances of winning or breaking even on the hand. Remember, the dealer only wins the original wager if he has blackjack.

10. You have a pair of ten-point cards. Decision: *Stand*. You should never alter a hand that has an excellent potential to be a winner.

Of the 330 possible point count combinations that can occur, based on the player's first two cards and the dealer's exposed card, 283 hands are included in the ten recommendations listed above, which accounts for 86 percent of all initial playing decisions that must be made by the player.

Consequently, about four-fifths of all initial playing decisions can be made by following the preceding suggestions!

Differences of Opinion

◆   Of the 330 potential decisions that a player must make when using Basic Strategy, there are forty-seven card combinations where the experts don't all agree as to which action should be taken.

Although contradictory advice only involves 15 percent of the possible hands, the choice made can easily be the difference between being a winner or loser. The differences of opinion and advice involve the following hands:

1. The player holds a hard point count of 8, while the dealer has an exposed 5 or 6. The majority of the experts advise hitting the hand, while three aggressive "experts" feel that doubling-down is worth the risk.

2. The player has a hard 9 against the dealer's exposed 2. The majority recommend hitting, while several instruct the player to double-down.

3. The player holds a hard 11, facing any card held by the dealer. A major difference of opinion exists when this situation occurs. Six of the experts recommend hitting against any card held by the dealer, while seven experts say double-down against any dealer card but the ace, in which case hitting would be the proper strategy.

4. The player has A/2 or A/3, while the dealer holds an exposed 4 or 5. The majority suggest hitting against the 4 and doubling against the 5, while the minority suggest just the opposite! It appears that the odds are so close that either decision may be appropriate.

5. The player has A/4 or A/5, and the dealer has a 4 or 5 exposed. The majority of the writers advise doubling-down in this situation, while several suggest only hitting the hand.

6. The player holds A/6, and the dealer shows a 3, 4, or 5. The majority recommend doubling-down, while the minority suggest hitting when the dealer shows 3, and standing against the dealer's 4 or 5. The minority seem to have taken a conservative position in this situation, not choosing to disrupt a soft 17 when facing a dealer's "stiff" cards.

7. The player has A/7, while the dealer has 2 through 6, or 9 through A. Great differences of opinion occur when the player holds A/7. Most experts suggest that the player double-down

against the 2 through 6, while the minority recommend standing. The majority advise hitting against the dealer's 9 through A, while the minority advise standing.

The minority rationale seems to be that the player should not attempt to improve a soft 18, while the majority opinion is that doubling or hitting will help the hand.

8. The player holds 2/2 or 3/3, and the dealer has a 2 or 3 exposed. Most experts say split the hand, while the minority say hit only.

While the odds may favor the player by splitting, the conservative minority do not seem to believe that doubling the wager is worth the risk.

9. The player holds 4/4 while the dealer shows a 5 or 6. The majority say hit only, but several experts disagree with the adage, "Never split fours!" and instruct the player to do so in this situation.

10. The player has 6/6, and the dealer shows 2 through 6. The majority instruct the player to split the 6s, while the minority suggest hitting against the 2 or 3, and standing against the 4, 5, or 6. Once again, several experts take a conservative position and don't feel that the player's hand justifies a doubling of the amount of the wager.

11. The player has 7/7, facing the dealer's 8. Most experts suggest splitting the hand, while the minority recommend hitting. The majority opinion seems to be that the split will result in at least one hand reaching a total of 18 or better, resulting in a no-loss situation, while the minority of the experts recommend only risking the original wager.

12. The player holds 9/9, facing the dealer's 8 or 9. Most experts instruct the player to split the 9s, in anticipation of winning both hands; the minority opinion is that 18 is a good hand and should not be altered in this situation.

still a game of chance, in spite of the experts' efforts to give sound advice to those who purchase their books.

"Keep It Simple, Stupid!"

◆ The preceding basic strategy chart describes every playing decision possible, but trying to memorize 330 different correct decisions might be asking too much of a novice player.

Therefore, a simplified chart, containing only the majority opinions, is presented below.

Simplified Basic Strategy Chart for Multideck Game (Double-Down After Split Permitted)

Dealer's Up-Card

Your Hand	2	3	4	5	6	7	8	9	10	A
5, 6, 7, or 8	H	H	H	H	H	H	H	H	H	H
9	H	D	D	D	D	D	H	H	H	H
10	D	D	D	D	D	D	D	D	H	H
11	D	D	D	D	D	D	D	D	D	H
12	H	H	S	S	S	H	H	H	H	H
13, 14, 15, 16	S	S	S	S	S	H	H	H	H	H
17, 18, 19	S	S	S	S	S	S	S	S	S	S
A/2 OR A/3	H	H	H	D	D	H	H	H	H	H
A/4 OR A/5	H	H	D	D	D	H	H	H	H	H
A/6	H	D	D	D	D	H	H	H	H	H
A/7	S	D	D	D	D	S	S	H	H	H
A/8 OR A/9	S	S	S	S	S	S	S	S	S	S
A/A	P	P	P	P	P	P	P	P	P	P
2/2	P	P	P	P	P	H	H	H	H	H
3/3	P	P	P	P	P	P	H	H	H	H
4/4	H	H	H	H	H	H	H	H	H	H
5/5	D	D	D	D	D	D	D	D	H	H
6/6	P	P	P	P	P	H	H	H	H	H
7/7	P	P	P	P	P	P	P	H	H	H
8/8	P	P	P	P	P	P	P	P	P	P
9/9	P	P	P	P	P	S	P	P	S	S
10/10	S	S	S	S	S	S	S	S	S	S

H = Hit   S = Stand   D = Double-Down   P = Split

Practice, Practice, Practice!

◆   Prior to playing in a casino, practice the rules and Basic Strategy by creating your own blackjack game.

All you need are six decks of standard playing cards and coins or chips to represent wagers placed by players. You can play the roles of both the players and the dealer.

Place six separate wagers for the players, and deal to each position as explained in the basic rules chapter. *Do not* look at the dealer's down-card, as this may affect your playing decisions.

Play each hand, using the strategy charts in this chapter. Keep practicing until you can make playing decisions without referring to the chart.

At the end of each shoe, keep track of the wins and losses experienced at each playing position. To keep it simple, bet only one unit (one chip) at the start of each hand.

Later on you can apply some of the progressive betting systems and table tactics suggested in later chapters of this book.

If you own a computer, purchase one of the inexpensive casino blackjack programs, and practice with it.

Remember, it is absolutely vital that you have a complete understanding of the rules and basic strategy of the game prior to learning the other aspects of play that are explained in upcoming chapters.

If you want to test your knowledge of the basic strategy decisions that will improve your chances of winning, take the following quiz. Don't peek at the answers at the end of the following quiz, and review this chapter if you didn't answer all of the questions correctly.

Basic Strategy Quiz

1. Your hand totals seven points. The dealer's exposed card is a 6. You should:

   a. Hit
   b. Stand   •
   c. Split
   d. Double-down

2. Your hand totals 15. The dealer has a 2 exposed. You should:
   a. Hit
   b. Stand
   c. Split
   d. Double-down

3. Your hand is king/7. The dealer has a queen exposed. You should:
   a. Hit
   b. Stand
   c. Split
   d. Double-down

4. Your hand is ace/3. The dealer's exposed card is a 7. You should:
   a. Hit
   b. Stand
   c. Split
   d. Double-down

5. Your hand is ace/8. The dealer shows a queen. You should:
   a. Hit
   b. Stand
   c. Split
   d. Double-down

6. Your hand is ace/ace. The dealer shows a 9. You should:
   a. Hit
   b. Stand

    c. Split
    d. Double-down

7. Your hand is a pair of 8s. The dealer's exposed card is a 9. You should:
    a. Hit
    b. Stand
    c. Split
    d. Double-down

8. Your hand is two face cards. The dealer shows a 6. You should:
    a. Hit
    b. Stand
    c. Split
    d. Double-down

9. Your hand is a pair of 6s. The dealer shows an 8. You should:
    a. Hit
    b. Stand
    c. Split
    d. Double-down

10. Your hand is a pair of 4s. The dealer's up-card is a 10. You should:
    a. Hit
    b. Stand
    c. Split
    d. Double-down

Answers to Basic Strategy Quiz:

   1. a   2. b   3. b   4. a   5. b   6. c   7. c   8. b   9. a   10. a

Card Counting

"The harder I work, the luckier I get."
—SAMUEL GOLDWIN

Once a player has mastered the basic rules of the game and has a clear understanding of basic strategy and money management, he may wish to take advantage of another tool designed to improve his chances of winning—a playing strategy known as *card counting*.

Blackjack is unlike most other casino games because the knowledgeable player has opportunities to predict the cards being dealt based on the previous cards that have been dealt.

The following example explains this concept:

You are playing against the dealer, "head to head," at a one-deck table. You know that the deck contains fifty-two cards—four aces, sixteen ten-point cards, and thirty-two cards ranging in value from two to nine points.

As play begins, you take note of the first card discarded by the dealer, and, as play progresses, the point value of every other card dealt to you and the dealer.

After thirty-six cards have been played and exposed, you recall that all four aces and thirty-one cards with values of two to nine points have been dealt.

On the next hand, you have a $100 bet at risk, are dealt two cards (face down), and the dealer's exposed card is the nine of diamonds. Without looking at your cards, what should you do?

The answer is obvious to the expert card counter: Split the hand, and continue splitting as long as the casino allows you to do so. You don't even have to look at your cards! You will win every hand! By keeping track of every card previously played, you know that when the current hand began, the *remaining cards* in the deck consisted of one nine-point card and sixteen ten-point cards. The dealer received the nine-point card as his exposed card. Consequently, his hole card *must* be a ten-point card, and your hand *must* be two ten-point cards, giving you a twenty to the dealer's count of nineteen.

More importantly, you know that *every other card in the remainder of the deck* is a ten-point card, and no matter how many times you split, your final hands will all equal twenty points! You are also breaking a cardinal rule of basic strategy by splitting tens, but since your knowledge of the value of the cards remaining in the deck is indisputable, this rule *must* be broken.

The preceding situation is the card counter's ultimate fantasy, and will probably never occur in an actual game of blackjack, but it does illustrate how card counting can affect your potential profits and how basic strategy rules are altered by the player's knowledge of the cards remaining in the deck.

A basic premise of card counting is that a deck that is "rich" in face cards and aces (a disproportionately high percentage of these cards) favors the player over the dealer. This is true for several reasons:

1. A player receiving a "natural," an ace and a ten-point card, is paid 3 to 2 on his original bet, whereas the dealer only wins the original wager if he has blackjack.

2. If the dealer receives a poor hand as his original two cards (a point count of twelve to sixteen, he must draw another card and is more likely to bust if the deck is rich in face cards.

On the other hand, the player has the option of ignoring basic strategy guidelines and not drawing to a "stiff" hand when the chances of busting are much greater than normal.

3. The chance of a higher than normal number of "push" hands exists, but no money is lost in these situations.

The card counter who experiences a deck that is rich in face cards and aces is advised to *increase* his unit bet, since his chances of winning are greater than normal.

Card counters also gain by knowing when the remaining cards in the deck are "poor" in face cards and aces:

1. The chances of drawing to a stiff hand are improved if fewer face cards are present, but the dealer shares the same advantage.

2. The player may choose to modify his split and double-down decisions when the number of low value cards far outnumber the face cards and aces, since the chances of winning these hands are reduced when a low card is dealt to the player after a split or double-down.

Players who are card counters normally bet their smallest wagers when the deck is rich in low point cards, since their chances of winning are reduced.

Card Counting Systems

There are many different techniques that have been researched and invented to keep track of the cards played from a deck or shoe. The object of all of the systems is the same: *to determine when the normal distribution of cards fails to occur; to determine when an abnormal number of high or low cards still remain to be dealt.* As soon as an abnormal flow of cards occurs, the player is advised to alter his wager and basic strategy tactics to take advantage of the "rich" or "poor" status of the remaining cards in the deck or shoe.

If a standard deck of fifty-two cards is shuffled and dealt, two possible extremes could occur:

A. The first twenty cards dealt could theoretically be all of the ten-point cards and aces, eliminating all high point cards from those remaining to be dealt.

B. The first thirty-two cards dealt could have a point count of two to nine points each, leaving only ten-point cards and aces to be dealt.

The card counter may never experience these two extreme possibilities, but uses one or more of the systems explained in this chapter to determine when the cards remaining in the deck are biased in one direction or the other.

An important point to remember about card counting is that a player using a *progressive betting system* will have little need for the betting techniques applied by card counters. Progressive betters generally follow their system automatically, regardless of the rich or poor condition of the remaining cards in the deck or shoe. In the section of this book that explains progressive betting systems, the possibility of incorporating these two philosophies will be discussed.

The various systems for counting cards are explained below, from the most simple to the more complex. Detailing and describing the required alterations in wagering and basic strategy are beyond the scope of this offering, but are available in many of the titles listed in the bibliography.

"Casual Counting"

The simplest form of card counting is easy to learn, requires no mathematical calculations, and demands little use of memory. Many novice players use this system without knowing they are doing so.

All that the player must do is observe the exposed cards on the table during and at the conclusion of one or more hands. A full table (six or seven players) is preferred since more cards are exposed on each deal.

This system only requires the player to casually observe how many high cards (ten through ace) are dealt. Assuming that six players and the dealer will use up twenty to twenty-five cards per hand, and knowing that 40 percent of the cards in a deck are high cards, the player should be able to look at the exposed cards and get a feeling for the mix of cards remaining to be dealt.

In a normally distributed deck, eight to ten of the twenty to twenty-five exposed cards should be *high* cards. If only four high cards should appear, the remainder of the deck will have a higher than normal percentage of high cards. Since this helps the player more than the dealer, a higher than normal bet may be advisable on the next hand.

If over twelve high cards are exposed, the remainder of the deck will have a *lower* than normal percentage of high cards (unfavorable to the player) and the player may choose to reduce his unit bet on the next hand.

In games involving four to six decks, the player may wish to count the number of high cards exposed over a two- or three-hand sequence.

The key to this system is to look for *extremes*. The absence or predominance of exposed high cards is easily noticeable through casual observation.

The chart below describes a possible card count for a four-deck shoe with six players at the table:

First Hand—3 high cards exposed
Second Hand—3 high cards exposed
Third Hand—2 high cards exposed
Total High Cards Exposed = 8
Total Cards Exposed = 80
Total Cards Remaining = 128

If the cards had been equally distributed throughout the deck, a total of thirty-two high cards should have been included among the first eighty cards dealt.

Consequently, there are *twenty-four more high cards than normal* still remaining in the shoe, which creates a rich deck.

Conversely, if the first three hands only contained eight low cards (two through nine), when forty-eight would have been dealt in a normally distributed shoe, there would be forty more low cards than normal still remaining to be dealt, making the shoe "poor" and unfavorable to the player.

In practice, it's easier to count high cards, since they stand out more clearly.

If the pattern of the cards dealt continues on the next hand (a low proportion of face cards being dealt) the advantage to the player increases, and another increase in the size of the wager would be in order, *even if the player were to have lost the previous hand.* All counting systems suggest that the bet be increased while playing conditions remain good or continue to improve, regardless of the financial success of the previous hand.

The amount of the bet is adjusted at the conclusion of each hand of play. If a large number of high cards are exposed following a small number of high cards exposed, the player advantage is eliminated and he should return to his original unit bet.

Many card counting experts suggest that the unit bet be increased from one to a maximum of four units, depending on deck conditions.

A typical series of hands could occur as follows (again, six players at a four-deck table):

Hand	High cards exposed	Total cards dealt	Wager
1	5	17	$5
2	5	16	$10
3	5	17	$15

Hand	High cards exposed	Total cards dealt	Wager
4	7	16	$20
5	10	14	$20
6	8	20	$5

You can see that the unit bet was increased until Hand 5, when a higher than normal percentage of face cards were exposed, thus wiping out the decided player advantage and causing the unit bet to be dropped to its original $5 level.

The odds of the player winning hands 2 through 5 were greater than normal, and the bet was increased to take advantage of the disproportionate cards favorable to the player. Once this advantage was wiped out, the wager was reduced to $5.

The casual counting system just described may be most helpful to a player who is new to the game and is still struggling to master rules and basic strategy, and, like all card counting systems, will only add a few percentage points of advantage to the long-term play of the game.

All other "respected" counting systems, such as the ones listed below, are based on computer simulations of the game of blackjack, and the increases and decreases in the size of the wager are like those illustrated in the preceding explanation.

Counting Fives

Early computer analysis of blackjack revealed that the player gains an advantage of almost 4 percent when *all* fives are removed from a single-deck game, because the dealer's chances of busting a stiff hand are better when no fives are available to be dealt.

The player is advised to increase his initial wager when a disproportionate number of fives have been played from a deck or shoe.

The Point Count System

One of the oldest and most popular card counting systems currently in use is the point count system (also known as the Hi-Lo), which is based on assigning a value of $+1$, 0, or -1 to every card dealt to all players and the dealer.

Most card counters suggest assigning a value of -1 to aces and ten-point cards, 0 (zero) to the 7, 8, and 9, and $+1$ to the 2, 3, 4, 5, and 6.

As cards are dealt, the player mentally keeps a running count of the cards, exposed, and makes wagering decisions based on the current total of the count:

> The higher the $+$ (plus) count, the higher the percentage of ten-point cards and aces remaining to be dealt, and the better the advantage to the player.
>
> If the running count remains near zero, the deck is neutral and neither the player nor the dealer has an advantage.
>
> The higher the $-$ (minus) count, the greater the disadvantage is to the player, since a higher percentage of high cards have already been dealt and a higher than normal number of "stiff" cards remain to be dealt.

As the deal progresses, the credibility of the count becomes more reliable, and the size of the player's wager can be increased or decreased with a higher probability of producing the anticipated results—betting and winning more when the deck is rich in face cards and aces, and betting and losing less when the deck is rich in "stiff" cards.

Alterations in basic strategy decisions are also recommended, based on the nature of the cards remaining to be dealt.

Many card counting proponents advise the player to increase the initial bet when the point count is $+2$ or more in a single deck game, and $+6$ or more in a multiple-deck game. The amount of the increase in the wager (from one to ten units higher than the previous bet) varies, depending upon the aggressiveness of the expert making the recommendation.

One of the most simple and yet most effective systems currently in use is the Hi-Opt 1 (an abbreviation for highly optimum) devised by Lance Humble and based on IBM computer programs developed by Julian Braun (see Bibliography). Simply stated, this system assigns a value of +1 to the 3, 4, 5, and 6, and −1 to the 10, jack, queen, and king. All other cards are ignored. The player keeps a running + or − count of all exposed cards, and bases his next wager on the current count.

Any increase in the unit bet is equal to the plus count at any given time during the dealing of a deck or shoe, after adjusting for the number of cards or decks remaining to be dealt.

For example, if the player has a running count of +6 after three decks have been dealt from a six-deck shoe, he gets a "true" count by dividing the running count by the number of remaining decks (+6 divided by 3 = 2) and bets two units as his next wager. He recalculates after each hand, and bets according to the true count, disregarding whether he won or lost the previous hand.

For a much more detailed explanation of Hi-Opt 1, I refer you to doctors Humble and Cooper's book, *The World's Greatest Blackjack Book*.

Long- and Short-Term Results of Play

Card counting proponents claim that the player will experience a definite advantage by applying their methods of play over a long period of time. Most experts estimate that each + or − count amounts to about a one-half percent advantage or disadvantage to the player. When specific table conditions and liberal rules exist, the card counter with a true count of +3 or more may experience a temporary statistical advantage over the house.

An excellent explanation of the potential win or loss rate, based on both short- and long-term play, is well presented by Stanford Wong, an internationally recognized expert in the mathematical analysis of blackjack. His 1975 book, *Professional Blackjack*, has been republished many times, and was written to assist the expert card counter.

He conducted computer studies, using standard blackjack rules, a six-deck table, and current playing conditions with two players at the table. The two players were dealt *600 million hands!*

The two computer-simulated players were required to wager $10 on initial or negative count hands, $25 if the point count was zero or +1, $50 if the point count was +2, $75 if the count was +3, and $100 if the count was +4 or more. They used the point count system previously described, (2, 3, 4, 5, 6 = +1; 7, 8, 9 = 0; ten, jack, queen, king, ace = −1).

The anticipated rule of play was estimated at one hundred hands per hour per player, and the *long-term results* showed a win rate of $16 per hour (one hundred hands) of play, give or take $.20 per hour (sampling error).

Does this mean that if you are an expert card counter, and wager $10 to $100 per hand, you will win $16 per hour. The answer is:

◆ *Yes*, if you play 600 million hands of blackjack with the rules and conditions previously described. If you play one-hundred hands per hour, you would have to play blackjack twenty-four hours a day, seven days a week, 365 days a year, for over 650 years!

No, if you play the game for a few hours, a few days, or a few years!

The key to this statistical analysis is the *standard deviation* per one hundred hands of play. Computer studies of repeated samples of one hundred hands of play indicated that *two-thirds* of the samples had wins of $16 *plus or minus $415!*

In other words, a typical hour of expert play could result in a profit of $431 or a loss of $431 *about two-thirds of the time!*

Stanford Wong also discovered that in a one-deck game, when only half of the deck was dealt, the win rate was $48 per hour (compared to $16 in a six-deck game), and the standard deviation was $482 per one hundred hands of play (compared to $431 in a six-deck shoe). Obviously, card counters have a higher long-term win rate at one-deck tables, but may experience a higher win or loss rate in short-term play.

♦   If you're in the game for the long term—six hundred years or so—card counting will work for you! If you don't have that much time, try following Basic Strategy, progressive betting, and table tactics recommendations suggested in other chapters of this book.

Practicing Card Counting

To practice how to learn a point counting system, start by using one deck of cards. Shuffle the deck, and deal one card at a time, face up. If using the point count system, assign the proper value of −1 (aces and ten-point cards), 0 (7, 8, and 9), or +1 (2, 3, 4, 5, or 6) to each card as it is dealt.

After dealing the entire deck, your point count should equal *zero*, since the value assigned to high cards equals the value assigned to low cards, and the 7, 8, and 9 have no point value. If the count doesn't equal zero, you made a mistake in your count and must start over.

If using the Hi-Opt 1 system, use the + and − values assigned to the eight cards that you are counting. Again, your end count should equal zero.

Keep practicing with a single deck until you can deal all the cards in less than ninety seconds without making a counting error. After perfecting the use of a single deck, add more cards until you can count six decks and come up with a count of zero after dealing the last card.

Next, deal seven simulated hands—six to players, and the dealer's hand—and keep a running count under actual playing conditions. If you can play out the entire six-deck shoe, and end with a running count of zero, you have gained the skill of being an expert card counter!

This point count system and the Hi-Opt 1 were devised about twenty-five years ago as a spin off from computer-generated basic strategy, and were very successful for knowledgeable players when first applied. Most casinos played blackjack with one deck, and dealt to the end of the deck before reshuffling, giving an occasional advantage to the card counter.

Unfortunately, casino executives soon learned how and why these and other systems worked, and took countermeasures to offset the advantage to the players.

They began by discouraging the play of those they believed to be card counters, often banning them from further play in their casinos. They introduced multiple deck games, and only dealt half the deck, or reshuffled after every hand in single deck games if card counting was suspected. The majority of the rule changes intended to alter the advantages of card counting are still in effect today.

Every year or so, new and "unique" card counting systems are introduced. These new systems are more complex and difficult to learn and apply than the counting systems previously explained, but are essentially only refinements on systems developed over two decades ago.

If the concept and potential benefits of card counting fascinates you, read some of the books listed in the Bibliography at the back of this volume.

Based on current playing conditions in today's casinos, I feel that card counting is generally a waste of time and effort.

I learned and practiced card counting many years ago, and came to the following conclusions:

1. The point count required to justify an increase in my bet only occurred about 25 percent of the time; 75 percent of my

effort and concentration resulted in no change in the amount that I wagered.

2. High positive point count hands often ended in "push" situations, where both the dealer and I received twenty-point hands.

3. I continued to use a progressive betting system while counting cards, and discovered that my wager was already higher when my point count was positive. Obviously I was winning consecutive hands because the point count was in my favor, regardless of the fact that I was counting cards!

4. After about one hour of play at the tables, I experienced headaches and mental fatigue caused by the concentration and eye strain (I wear bifocals!) required by card counting.

5. Altering my basic strategy decisions was almost impossible! Once I had learned to play by these proven principles, the recommendation to change them was very difficult.

6. I play blackjack for recreation, and realized that all of my efforts were focused on counting cards. I wasn't having any fun!

◆   One more observation about card counting: Many expert counters and writers who proclaim the benefits of counting systems claim that the player must *disguise his card counting skills.* Otherwise, the casinos will discourage or disallow you from playing blackjack.

I've spent thousands of hours at blackjack tables all over the United States and in the Bahamas. I've *never once* seen a player harassed or ejected because he was a card counter.

On the other hand, on many occasions I've seen players experience casino pressure or ejection for reasons *other* than card counting, such as being drunk, belligerent, uncouth, or attempting to cheat.

I've personally experienced many of the tactics that casino managers use to disrupt the concentration and/or good luck of a knowledgeable player on a winning streak. These tactics, such as changing dealers, changing to new decks, slowing or speeding up the dealing of the game, cutting the shoe much more shallow than usual, reshuffling more often, and other measures were attempted to change my good fortune.

I have also noticed that these changes in the flow of the game never seem to occur when I'm losing!

Again, I've never personally seen or heard of a player who was harassed simply because he was a card counter.

I *do* believe that the "casual counting" system described in this chapter can be advantageous to most players, because the absence of face cards spread over the table is so blatantly obvious. It requires no serious concentration to observe that only two or three face cards appeared over the course of a dozen hands being dealt, and it's simple to add a chip or two to the next wager.

The presence of *many* face cards on the table is also obvious, and should tell the player that a bet reduction on the next hand might be wise.

If you have problems with accepting the validity of betting systems, some of which are described in the next chapter, card counting offers a reasonable rationale for increasing the size of your bet, based on mathematical probability rather than wild hunches.

"Cluster Counting" or "Shuffle Tracking"

Recently a new method of determining the probability of a higher than normal percentage of high cards being dealt is being promoted by writers of blackjack books.

This method of counting is based on the assumption that cards tend to "cluster" in certain parts of a multiple deck shoe, and that standard methods of shuffling the cards at the conclusion of a shoe can be "tracked" by the player so that he can determine which portions of the next shoe will be rich in player-friendly cards. This counting method consists of the following steps:

1. Begin observing the flow of cards at the start of a new shoe, while mentally dividing the shoe into sections equal to one deck.

2. Count the number of aces and ten-point cards that are dealt from each section of the shoe, with the objective being to ascertain if any portion of the shoe is rich in high cards.

3. Rate each section as being rich or poor, and note how cards are placed in the discard box.

4. At the conclusion of the shoe (assuming that at least 75 percent of the shoe was dealt), watch how the dealer shuffles the new shoe. Keep track of where the clusters of high cards are located, and where they will surface in the dealing of the next shoe.

5. Based on your observations, increase your wager when you reach those sections of the shoe that are rich in high point cards; decrease your wager when the deck is rich in "stiff" cards.

◆ Personally, I find this system to be much too difficult for the average player to master. The effort required to make it work is almost mind-boggling! The player must watch every card dealt, watch the shuffle, and remember where high cards may be located, and at the same time apply strategy, betting techniques, and proper table tactics.

Also, casino personnel, responding to the *possibility* that cluster counting might be effective, have begun counter-measures by changing the pattern of the shuffle, using two discard racks, and by installing automated shuffling machines.

The quiz on the following pages will test your knowledge of the factual information contained in this chapter. If you have an interest in becoming a sophisticated card counter, study some of the specialized books related to this subject. Proponents still claim that a player will experience a 2 to 3 percent long-term advantage over the house by properly counting and wagering.

Card Counting Quiz
(Select the *best* answer)

1. If you are playing at a two-deck table, and eleven ten-point cards were dealt in the first three rounds of play, how many ten-point cards are still available to be dealt?
   a. 19
   b. 21
   c. 29
   d. 16

2. The purpose of counting cards is to determine if:
   a. The remaining cards are "rich" in high cards.
   b. The remaining cards are "poor" in high cards.
   c. The remaining cards are neither rich nor poor in high cards.
   d. All of the above.

3. If the deck is rich in ten-point cards, the card counting player should:
   a. Decrease his next bet.
   b. Increase his next bet.
   c. Leave his bet unchanged.
   d. Leave the table.

4. A deck of shoe that is poor in ten-point cards:
   a. Favors the dealer.
   b. Favors the player.
   c. Favors neither the dealer nor the player.
   d. Tells the player to increase his bet.

5. The object of all card counting systems is:
   a. To determine when the normal distribution of high and low cards fails to occur.
   b. To determine when an abnormal number of high or low cards still remain to be dealt.
   c. To determine when the next wager should be increased or decreased.
   d. All of the above.

6. A player who expertly counts cards:
   a. Gains a major advantage over the casino.
   b. Gains a minor advantage over the casino.
   c. Is likely to win 95 percent of the hands that he plays.
   d. Uses a "flat" betting system.

7. Casual counting:
   a. Is one of the simplest forms of card counting.
   b. Requires that the players only count the ten-point cards that have been dealt.
   c. Requires that the player look for *extremes* in the distribution of cards.
   d. All of the above.

8. Which of the following is *not* a card counting system?
   a. Counting fives.
   b. The point count system.
   c. Casual counting.
   d. The Martingale System.

9. A player using a point count system:
   a. Assigns a value of $+1$ to aces and ten-point cards.
   b. Assigns a value of -1 to the 2, 3, 4, 5, and 6.

   c. Assigns a value of "0" to 7, 8, and 9.
   d. All of the above.

10. In order to counteract the benefits of card counting, casinos can:
   a. Increase the number of decks being used.
   b. Reshuffle up more often.
   c. Use a much more shallow cut in a multiple deck game.
   d. All of the above.

Answers to Card Counting Quiz

1. b   2. d   3. b   4. a   5. d   6. b   7. d   8. d   9. c   10. d

Betting Systems

"Winning is not everything. It's the only thing."
—VINCE LOMBARDI

The purpose of this chapter is to explain *if* or *when* you should increase or decrease the size of your blackjack bet.

Winning money is the object of this game; not losing money is almost as important. If you don't bet properly, your chances of accomplishing either of these goals is almost nonexistent.

Most blackjack tables allow the player a wide range of latitude in the amount that can be wagered on each hand. The minimum and maximum allowable wager is posted at each table, with the maximum bet normally being twenty to forty times the amount of the minimum bet (Examples: $5 to $200, $25 to $500). Some tables have maximum wagers ranging from $2000 to $5000.

The player may wager the minimum, the maximum, or any amount in between as his initial wager on each hand dealt.

If the player should split or double-down, he is allowed to exceed the table limit in order to match his previous bet.

Since blackjack is a game where betting systems applied by an expert have a chance of generating substantial profits, a thorough understanding of the various systems is essential.

These systems are designed to accomplish specific goals, such as directing the player to wager a higher amount when his chances of winning are better, or suggesting that the player place his bets in such a manner that new wagers won offset previous wagers lost.

Card counting, as explained in a previous chapter, includes a betting system as part of its philosophy. The player is advised to increase his unit bet up to four or more times his initial unit bet when conditions favor his winning the hand.

Some of the more well-known systems, and their potential shortcomings, are explained below:

The Martingale System

This system, invented in the late 1700s, instructs the player to *double* his bet each time he loses, on the assumption that he will eventually win and show a profit from the initial wager.

A typical betting sequence, after each loss, would be as follows: $5, $10, $20, $40, $80, $160, etc. The bet would remain the same ($5) each time a hand is won. All lost wagers are recovered when a hand eventually wins.

Faults: Table limits are specifically designed to eliminate the effectiveness of systems like Martingale. On a $5 table with a $200 maximum bet limit, a player would no longer be allowed to double his previous bet after losing *six* hands in a row. His last losing wager would be $160, and he would be disallowed from making a $320 bet due to the table limit of $200, thus destroying the whole principle behind the system.

The d'Alembert System

Jean Le Rond d'Alembert, a French mathematician, invented this system in the eighteenth century. The player begins by betting one unit. Each time he loses, he increases his bet by one unit. Each time he wins, he decreases his bet by one unit. The object is to return to the one unit bet, assuring the player of a profit.

Faults: The d'Alembert is not as dangerous as the Martingale because the required bet increases are not as severe, but it still requires the player to increase his bets while losing, thus threatening his bankroll and facing the maximum table limit dilemma.

Also, with both of the preceding systems the player's bankroll can be severely damaged if he should lose a split or double-down hand when large sums are being wagered. Additionally, both systems require that the player *increase* his bet after losing—not an easy thing to do for most players.

♦ These two systems, the Martingale and the d'Alembert, have both been periodically "reinvented" by writers and self-appointed experts for the last two hundred years or so. They would show consistently profitable results if the player had an unlimited bankroll and the casino placed no limit on the maximum amount that could be wagered on a single hand, which is not the case.

These systems can also be profitable in the short run, if the player *wins more hands than he loses,* but so can *any other type of betting system* that increases the amount of the original wager. Even betting the same amount on each and every hand (a "flat" bet) will result in a profit if you are winning more hands than you are losing. The odds of this happening are poor, as is explained in other chapters of this book, so you may wish to give serious consideration to the progressive betting systems described below.

Progressive Betting Systems

♦ There are several schools of thought regarding progressive betting—automatic increases in the size of the wager after winning a hand.

Many experts, especially those that are card counters, feel that a "flat" bet (the same amount on every hand) should be wagered until the point count favors the player, at which time the bet should be increased from two to ten times the original amount.

Other experts suggest that basic strategy players should only increase their wagers for three or four consecutive winning hands, since the odds of winning a large number of consecutive hands are slim.

Still other experts recommend using a *regressive* progressive system which instructs the player to reduce his first winning wager by one half, and then increase the bet by one unit after each consecutive winning hand. This system allows the player a profit if he wins the first hand and loses the second hand.

Fault: The player's overall profit is reduced if he wins consecutive hands.

Another type of system, proposed by Donald Dahl and others (see the Bibliography) instructs the player to increase his bets *as he is winning*, and return to the original unit bet only when he loses. The suggested betting progressions vary, but might be like this (all winning wagers):

$5, $5, $10, $10, $15, $15, etc.

or

$5, $7, $9, $11, $15, $20, etc.

or

$10, $15, $20, $25, $30, etc.

If at any time a split or double-down hand is won, the player is instructed to "jump" one level, because he won at least twice as much at the previous level.

In the event of a loss, the bet reverts to the one-unit level. No change occurs with a push hand.

The obvious advantage of this system is that the player wins ever-increasing amounts when he is on a winning streak, and loses only the minimum wager while on a losing streak Also, the system is simple to follow and requires no mathematical skill; simply add one or two units to each winning hand, and revert to the original unit bet after a loss.

Another advantage is that the player is often using "house money" (cash he didn't have when he entered the casino) to risk on winning additional profits. One or two extended streaks of winning hands can be very profitable, and can quickly offset a series of losing streaks where only the minimal bets were lost.

Faults: As in all other systems, the player can lose consistently if the cards are running against him. Short-run fluctuations can defeat the best player at any time.

Also, the player's profits from positive progressive betting can be wiped out by the loss of split or double-down hands.

◆ In spite of these hazards, I strongly believe in the effectiveness of this type of system, and use progressive betting as an integral part of my game, as is described in a later chapter.

My wife, my mother, and several of my friends also follow this system, as do many professional gamblers. While they don't always win, they seldom lose very much!

Table Tactics

"If you live among wolves you have to act like a wolf."
—Nikita Krushchev

◆ Having learned the rules of blackjack and basic strategy, the theory of card counting, and the basics of betting systems, it's now time to get to the meat of the issue—playing the game in a casino.

I consider this chapter to be of vital importance to the success of every player, and recommend that the tactics explained below be integral elements of every playing session.

Select the Best Casino   Play this game in casinos that have liberal rules, a wide range of minimum and maximum bet limits, enough open tables to allow easy movement from one table to the next, a comfortable environment, reasonably priced food, lodging, and entertainment, friendly personnel, and a comp program that appreciates your being there.

If the casino you selected doesn't offer most of these conditions, go elsewhere!

Play Where You Feel Comfortable   If you like a flashy, fast-paced, hectic environment, play at a casino that offers this atmosphere. If you prefer a slower-paced, quiet, sedate environment, find a facility that offers these conditions. Don't play where you are physically or mentally uncomfortable.

Tour the Facility Before You Begin Play   The exterior of a casino doesn't necessarily reflect the conditions present on the casino floor. The cool chandeliered lobby full of antique furniture may lead you to a crowded, smoke-filled, hot, grimy casino manned by surly dealers and pit bosses.

Plan Your Time Schedule Before Beginning Play   I can't tell you how many arguments I've witnessed at the blackjack table because a husband (or wife) failed to leave the game in time for dinner or show reservations.

Be Sure That You Are Physically Rested and Mentally Prepared Before Starting to Play   Most visitors to casinos travel many hours by plane, bus, or car prior to arrival, often reach their destination late at night, go through the hustle and bustle of check-in and unpacking, and then head directly to the casino. Don't do it! A mentally and physically exhausted player is often a poor player. It takes a considerable amount of concentration, physical stamina, and emotional control to play this game successfully. Don't handicap yourself before you even begin playing.

Select a Potentially Winning Table   Once you are ready to play and feel comfortable with the environment, try to find a table where your chances of winning might be good.

As you look at a table, do the players seem to be enjoying themselves? Do they have stacks of chips in front of them? Are they talking to each other, and to the dealer? Does the dealer seem to be enjoying dealing the game? These are some of the indications of a "player-friendly" table; if they are not present, seek another table.

Playing Tactics

◆　　Once you find a table that seems acceptable, there are several important actions that you should take before and during play.

Verify the Rules　　Many casinos have different rules of play from one table to the next. Be sure that you understand the rules at the table at which you are seated, and check each time you move to a different table.

I was recently in a casino in Reno, alternating between two tables in the same pit area. One table allowed doubling-down on 9, 10, or 11 only, while the other table allowed doubling-down on any two cards! Be sure that you know the rules at each table.

Don't Make Side Bets　　Casino owners have added a number of new betting options for blackjack players, ostensibly to "spice up" the game. The idea is to make a side bet (usually $1, placed in a slot in front of the betting box) based on the chances of the first one, two, or three cards received by the player being 7s, As, diamonds, or whatever.

The odds appear to be favorable (2 to 1, 5 to 1, 100 to 1). A flashy display placard showing the card combinations and payoff odds is provided to encourage players to make these side bets. *Don't do it!* The house enjoys a much higher percentage advantage on these bets than it does on the regular game. If your original unit bet is $5, why risk an additional wager equal to 20 percent of that amount ($1) when the odds of winning are much worse than in the regular game? You are better off to add the $1 to your unit bet.

It Doesn't Matter Where You Sit at the Table　　Many players are superstitious, and feel that they must play at the "post" position (the first seat to the dealer's left) or at the "anchor" or "third base" position (the last seat to the dealer's right). They feel that they can "control the flow" of the cards from these positions, or be less affected by the actions of other players.

In truth, many studies have proven that there is no difference in the long-term results of play based on seat location.

The only exception to this principle would occur if the player knew how to "peek." Peeking is the practice of seeing the dealer's hole card before it is exposed, and can occur when the dealer originally deals himself his hole card or when he must look at the hole card in advance to see if he has a "natural."

If the dealer is inexperienced or poorly trained, he may accidentally reveal the card by holding it too high off the table. The best angle from which to see this card would be from the post or anchor seat. Knowing the exact value of the dealer's hole card can obviously have a very positive effect on the outcome of the hand.

Incidentally, the dealer may occasionally make another mistake which will help any player at the table. In most cases the dealer is required to check his hole card if he has an exposed ten-point card and there is a "natural" (blackjack) on the table, or if he has an ace exposed and a player takes insurance. The 4 and the ace look much alike when "flashed" quickly. Consequently, if the dealer looks *twice* at his hole card, it's possible that his hole card is a low card.

Even though where you sit at the table doesn't have any long-term effect on wins or losses, I advise the *novice* player to sit as far to the dealer's right as possible. If your playing decisions require that you *think* about what you should do, you will be allowed more time since you are the last player at the table to receive cards. The extra few seconds will help until basic strategy decisions become natural to you.

Don't Try to Keep Up With the Dealer   Occasionally a player is faced with a dealer who chooses to deal *very* fast. This may occur because he has been instructed to do so by the pit boss in order to put pressure on a winning player, or it may be the natural preference of the dealer.

The rapid pace of play can be especially intimidating to a novice player. If this occurs, you can reduce the speed of play by taking a bit longer to signal your playing decision, or you can politely ask the dealer to slow down the game. If he doesn't do so, move to another table.

Don't Continue to Play at a Table Where You Feel Uncomfortable Any distraction that annoys you while playing this game can only hurt you, and a winning table can change to a losing table in the blink of an eye. A new dealer can be inserted, players may leave and be replaced by others, or the cards may take a drastic turn against you. Don't let yourself become too attached to a particular seat at a particular table.

You should be having fun while playing. The banter at the table should be an enjoyable experience, as you and the other players attempt to outwit and outdraw the dealer. If the other players (or the dealer) don't appreciate your presence, move to another table.

I've left winning tables on many occasions because I couldn't tolerate the personality of the dealer or other players.

The Playing Decisions Made By Other Players at the Table Have No Overall Effect on Your Winning or Losing This is one of the most difficult concepts for most players to accept. In truth, incorrect strategy decisions by other players will help you as often as they hurt you. We tend to remember the big hand that was lost when the player on our right hit his 16 against the dealer's 14, and we forget similar situations where the mistake led to a winning hand *In the long run, it makes no difference*, but if you are uncomfortable playing next to an unskilled player, move elsewhere.

Show Your Comp Card, or Ask to Be Rated, As Soon As You Sit Down at a Table Comps are based on the amount of time that you play as well as the amount of your average wager, and the sooner your presence at the table is recorded, the better your rating will be.

Control Your Negative Emotions Generally, the most unsuccessful player is the one who *expects* to lose. Many players form this attitude after losing several hands when the cards where statistically in their favor. Don't allow short-term bad luck to affect your playing skill or emotional control. If you expect to lose, why play?

Mind Your Own Business There are many players who feel that they are experts at the game, and want everyone else at the table to know it! They insist on telling others how to play, even when their advice is neither asked for nor appreciated. How can a player seriously concentrate on his own hand while he is busy playing everyone else's hand?

Make the Dealer Your "Friend" By being sociable and friendly, and tipping occasionally, it's possible to turn the dealer into an ally who is willing and often capable of helping you win more often.

These situations occur when the dealer has a face card exposed and he is required to look at his hole card prior to dealing the second round of cards. Assuming that you have convinced the dealer to be sympathetic, and that the pit boss is not watching too closely, he can provide many hints to tell you what he has in the hole.

Let's assume the following scenario:

You've won several hands in a row, have increased your bet to $50, and have placed a $5 bet for the dealer in your box. The dealer deals you a 9 and 7, and deals himself an exposed face card. Another player has blackjack, and the dealer then looks at his hole card to see if he has blackjack.

At this point, the helpful dealer can do several things which give you hints as to the nature of his hole card. Assuming he doesn't have blackjack, he may:

1. Look at the hole card *longer than usual*, telling you that the hole card may not be a face card, since "picture" cards only require a quick glance to be identified.

2. Look at the hole card *quicker* than usual (often just a quick "snap" of the thumb) indicating that the hole card is a face card.

3. Look at the card *more than once*, indicating that a low card may be in the hole, since "nonpaint" cards, especially the 4, look similar to an ace on a quick glance.

Back to our current hand:

The dealer looks at his hole card *twice*, and because you carefully watched his eyes and hands, you are fairly sure that his hole card is *not* a face card.

How the dealer goes about dealing you the next card can also tell you the probable nature of his hole card. Most experienced dealers recognize expert blackjack players by the way they play. They often *anticipate* that a player will automatically make a correct basic strategy decision.

Knowing that the dealer is aware of your knowledge of proper playing strategy, and noting that the dealer *ignores this fact*, or indicates that you should *not* follow basic strategy, can also help reveal the identity of his hole card. He may:

1. Begin dealing to you *before* you signal your desire to stand or hit your hand.

2. Hesitate dealing to you for a longer period of time than normal.

3. Ask you if you wish to take a card, even *after* you have made a hand signal!

Let's get back to our current hand:

Your exposed sixteen-point count still faces the dealer's exposed face card, but the dealer has previously indicated that he has something other than a face card in the hole. He also knows that you consistently hit 16 against a face card.

When it is your turn to receive a card, he *hesitates*, implying that your 16 may be a winner. You pretend to ponder the situation, and look the dealer in the eye. He says, "Do you wish a card, Sir?" but seems to mean, "You don't want a card."

You have now received *three* separate and distinct clues that indicate that the dealer has a "stiff" hand, and that you *should not* apply basic strategy and hit your 16. You stand on 16, the dealer reveals his hole card—a five—and draws a face card to bust his hand. He pays you $100, and doubles his $5 tip to $10. You give him the tip, and you both smile at each other. Isn't it a fun game when it works this way?

My best experience with great personal rapport with a dealer occurred on a stationary riverboat in Biloxi, Mississippi. The dealer was a middle-aged female who was extremely competent at her job. We were playing "head to head" and she quickly recognized that I was a knowledgeable player. I was winning moderately, and betting tips for her when my initial $25 wager reached a progressive bet of $50.

After about twenty minutes I was over two hundred dollars ahead and had $40 wagered. The hand was a "push," since we both had 18, but she accidentally paid me as a winner. I instinctively pointed out the mistake (I can't help it sometimes!) and a very unusual thing happened. She stopped the game and called the pit boss, who had been ignoring us due to the three high rollers at the next table. She explained her error, and emphasized that I had recognized the mistake and returned the unearned $40. He shook my hand, offered a free gourmet meal for me and my family, and a night's lodging at a nearby hotel, all in appreciation for my honesty! Since we were leaving that evening, I declined his generous offers. As he turned back to the high rollers, who were losing heavily, he told my dealer, "Take care of this man."

For the next forty-five minutes, I was in blackjack heaven! The pit boss ignored our table, which fortunately remained a head-to-head game, and the dealer did *everything possible* to help me win! When it was time for her break, I was $1,200 ahead, and she had $75 in tips. I thanked her and the pit boss for their "consideration," and left the casino.

What a great afternoon! As usual, honesty was the best policy.

It is not always necessary for the dealer to be your friend in order for you to learn the value of the dealer's hole card. On rare occasions, a novice or poorly trained dealer will inadvertently give many of the clues previously described. You must stay alert and observant if you wish to take advantage of these situations.

◆ THE TACTICS explained in this chapter will improve your chances of being a consistent winner at this game. Be sure to apply them.

Now that you know how and when to play this game, how much money do you need to have a good chance of winning? The next chapter addresses this question.

Money Management

*"The best way to double your money is to fold it
over once and put it in your pocket."*

—KEN HUBBARD

◆   The object of money management is to allow you to play the
game throughout the duration of your visit to a casino.

Most of the gambling experts tell the player to have twenty to
fifty times the amount of his initial unit bet when he begins a
"session" of play, but the explanation of the term "session" is
often confusing.

Some experts define a session as the amount of time it takes
to win a specific amount of money in relation to the size of the
bankroll.

Others refer to a session as a specific amount of time spent at
the table, such as forty-five minutes, one hour, four hours, etc.

Some writers instruct the player to quit playing after winning
a certain percentage of the original bankroll, or a specific multiple
of the original unit bet.

I define a gambling session as the amount of time that *you
personally plan to play blackjack*, and recommend the following
money management system:

Calculate the total bankroll required on the basis of the

amount of time you plan to spend sitting at a blackjack table. Allow at least twenty-five times your unit bet for each hour of play, assuming you are playing one hand at a full table.

Allow fifteen minutes each hour for interruptions in play (reshuffling, changing tables, restroom break, quick snack).

For instance, if your basic wager is $10, your bankroll should be:

> One Hour of Play = $250
> Four Hours of Play = $750
> Eight Hours of Play = $1,500
> Three-Night Trip = $4,500

If losses cause you to use up your hourly allotment of gambling money in less time, discontinue playing. Grab a bite to eat, see a show, go for a walk. If you exceed your bankroll limitations, you sacrifice future playing time. Also, one of the best ways to stop a losing streak is to stop playing!

I often gamble on one of several ships that depart on "cruises to nowhere" from the Fort Lauderdale area. Since I normally play two concurrent hands, with an initial two unit bet ($10) on each hand, I double the amounts suggested above, plan on four hours of play, and have a bankroll of $1,500.

I generally purchase $300 in chips at my first table, and occasionally never need to invest additional cash in the game.

On rare occasions, I lose my entire bankroll, and at other times I make a sizable profit for my efforts.

On trips to the major gambling centers, I travel with my family, spend less than six hours a day at the tables, and plan my bankroll accordingly.

It's very important that you realize that all gamblers, whether they be novices or experts, experience winning and losing sessions.

Stanford Wong conducted computer studies of over 200 million hands of blackjack, using the rules, card counting strategy, and betting system described in a previous chapter of this publication. The bets, based on + counts, were $5, $20, or $50 per hand.

After each 1,000 hands of play, the win or loss results were tabulated. The 1,000 hand series was repeated 20,000 times, and the results were as follows, as applied to a six-deck shoe:

1. The player was losing $100 or more, 87 percent of the time.
2. The player was losing $500 or more, 52 percent of the time.
3. The player was losing $1,000 or more, 22 percent of the time.

◆ Anybody who tells you that he always wins, or that you will always win by using his methods, is either a liar or a cheat.

The knowledgeable player should learn to properly respond to winning and losing streaks, and adjust his game to fit the situation.

When winning, I *increase my unit bet* when my profits from play equal forty times my initial bet ($400). I increase my initial wager to five units ($25) and increase in two-unit increments ($35, $45, etc.) until I reach a $100 maximum, which I play until I bust the hand.

If I lose some of my profits, and my winnings for the session decrease to twenty times my original $10 bet ($200), I drop back to the two-unit level.

Keep in mind that my system of playing blackjack will still result in more losing sessions than winning sessions in the long run (the odds still favor the house), but the amount of my winnings are often much greater than the amount of my losses. The object is to win more when you're winning and lose less when you're losing.

There are several other actions that you may wish to consider when you are winning, such as purchasing a cashier's check with your winnings and sending it to your home address, or leaving your profits in a safe in your room and going to the casino with only the amount required for the current session of play.

Beginning each new session of play by betting your original unit wager is also a good method of preserving your previous good fortune.

If you change tables after a winning streak, go to the cashier's cage and redeem some of your chips for cash. Remember, another objective of money management is to show a profit for your efforts. By putting cash in your wallet or purse, you take away the temptation of throwing those colorful chips back into the betting box.

When attempting to manage your gambling bankroll, you must have a clear understanding of how much of your money is available for gaming. How much money are you actually risking when you play blackjack, or any other casino game?

Casinos often advertise how little they supposedly make in profits, and display huge neon billboards indicating how they "return" 97.5 percent on slot machines, and "friendly" pit bosses will tell you that they only earn a 2 percent profit on blackjack, etc.

Since you are obviously interested in improving your knowledge about blackjack, you may have read books and articles that tell you that you can reduce an overall casino advantage of about 10 percent to 0 to 2 percent by learning basic strategy, and money management.

Many players may be under the impression that a 2 percent disadvantage means that they can expect to lose that percentage of their bankroll during a gambling session—about $2 per $100 of bankroll, compared to $10 per $100 for the unskilled player. If the difference is only a few dollars between just knowing the basic rules and being an expert player, why bother to do all of the homework?

In truth, the percentages of potential loss are very misleading, and are actually *much greater* than what might be anticipated.

Let's assume that a casino game makes an overall gross profit of 10 percent on a particular casino game. This means that in the long run (if there is only one player) or in the short run (if there are many players), the casino will make an average profit of 10 percent for *each and every bet made*. This 10 percent profit approximates the true amount that casinos earn from blackjack players who don't understand basic strategy, betting systems, card counting, and money management—the typical unskilled player.

Assuming this hypothetical percentage of 10 percent gross profit, let's examine what happens at a blackjack table:

You are a novice player, with a bankroll of $200, and are making flat bets of $5 per hand. The average dealer is capable of dealing you forty to one hundred hands per hour of play, depending on the number of players at the table and his speed at dealing the cards.

If you are playing forty hands per hour, and losing at a 10 percent rate, you will have wagered $200 in an hour, and lost $20. Your bankroll is now $180, and you continue playing.

Most casinos expect you to play at least four hours per day to be eligible for comps of food or lodging. To meet this require-ment, you continue play for three more hours, lose $20 per hour, and suffer an additional $60 reduction in your bankroll. When you quit play for the day, you've lost $80, *or 40 percent of your bankroll.*

If you had been averaging one hundred hands per hour, which is very possible in a head-to-head game with a fast dealer, *you would have lost your entire bankroll in the first hour of play.*

Isn't it interesting how your anticipated loss of $20 is really $80 to $200?

The reason to learn the information presented in this book

should be obvious: Reducing the house advantage from 10 percent to 0, to 2 percent might save you as much as $50 per hour of playing time, based upon the previous illustration.

If your flat bet was $25 per hand, the savings could be as much as $250 per hour!

It's your money, and your decision. Either do your homework, or help provide the funds to redecorate the lobby in the casino!

And remember, you can't experience the fun of playing this game if you are broke!

The Gambling Junket

"I spent most of my money on blackjack, booze, and beautiful women. The rest I just wasted."

—Anonymous

Planning a Gambling Vacation

◆   Preparation is the key to the success of any trip, especially one involving a major gambling area like Las Vegas or Atlantic City. Nothing you plan to do should be left to chance if you can possibly avoid it.

Based on my past experience, it's extremely frustrating to visit an area without advance planning, and then discover that your favorite casino/resort has no vacancies, the show you wish to see is sold out weeks in advance, rental cars are no longer available, the riverboat with the best blackjack tables moved to another location, your child's favorite theme park closed for renovations two months ago, your comp rating by the casino is no longer being honored due to a change in management, a new and much better casino/resort just opened across the street, you packed the wrong clothing, child care services no longer exist at your hotel, your favorite golf course is now a shopping mall, etc., etc., etc.!!!

77

Without advance planning, anything can go wrong, and probably will!

The following suggestions should make your gambling vacation more enjoyable:

Select a Definite Destination   Although this suggestion seems obvious, many travelers, especially those going by automobile or motor home, fail to plan their route or final destination. Seeing where the "wheels and the wind carry you" is a romantic and adventurous concept, but can lead to you sleeping in your car in a shopping center parking lot in ninety-degree heat!

Research the Gaming Facilities and Other Recreational Activities Available in the Area That You Plan to Visit   Later in this book you will find a list of many of the biggest and best casino resorts in the United States. Almost all of them have toll free telephone numbers, so call your "800" operator, get the numbers you need, and devote some serious time to making telephone calls. These establishments will be more than happy to send you brochures and other useful information about the area you plan to visit.

If you are visiting an area where a large number of casinos are available, call a number of them before deciding on a specific facility. Don't let past loyalties to a particular establishment dissuade you from trying out a new location, and the most expensive (or most economical) may not be the best for you and your friends or family. Decide in advance what you wish to experience in the time available to all of you, and select the location that will best fulfill these wishes.

Plan Your Trip and Make Reservations Well in Advance   Your travels may take you to many of the most popular vacation spots in the world. Many facilities are sold out months in advance. Seasonal fluctuations in certain areas caused by weather condi-

tions and major holidays may persuade you to visit at a different
time. If you don't like masses of people, and don't like standing in
line, don't visit Las Vegas on a holiday weekend when a major new
casino complex has just opened! Time lost waiting for space at a
blackjack table, or waiting in lines for lodging, meals, and other
recreational activities is very irritating to most vacationers, and
cuts into the short time that you have to do what you are paying
lots of money to do!

Ask About Comps, Rating Systems, and Fun Books   Many casinos
provide free or discounted food, lodging, or other services to
those who gamble with them. Determine the specific requirements you must meet to qualify for these "freebies."

Keep in mind that comp rating systems are normally based on
the amount of time that you gamble and the average amount of
your normal wager, not on whether you win or lose. To insure
that you receive any gratuities to which you are entitled, ask
about the rating system when you make your initial reservation
inquiries.

If possible, have the casino marketing department send you
written details and an identification card in your name. If you have
been previously rated by other casinos, determine if these ratings
allow you any immediate discounts. Remember, it costs nothing to
ask!

Insure Your Travel Expenses   If traveling by commercial carrier,
pay the additional fee to insure no loss to you if you have to
change or cancel your trip. It's worth the peace of mind.

Seek Out Other Information About Your Chosen Facility and Location-
Casinos tend to be self-centered when providing information
to prospective visitors; they often don't want you to know what
goes on *outside* the walls of their facility.

Fortunately, there are many travel guides available through local bookstores and specialty book distributors (see the Bibliography at the end of this book) that provide a wealth of information about the specific location that you are visiting.

Plan Your Wardrobe   Ask about local dress codes (although today almost anything goes!) and call for local weather conditions prior to departure.

I know from personal experience that it can be 20 degrees and snowing in Reno in late April, and 106 degrees in Las Vegas in early June!

Anticipate the Unexpected!   Think about what might go wrong, and determine how you might prepare for it in advance.

I can assure you that it is very difficult to purchase junior strength aspirin at 3:00 A.M. on a Sunday morning in Lake Tahoe!

Preplan the Use of Your Time   Based on all of the information that you gathered in advance, make a tentative schedule of the time you have available to do things other than playing blackjack! Recreational activities in gambling resort areas are some of the finest in the world, and are very reasonably priced. Don't miss out on the opportunity to experience them.

Separate Gambling Money From Travel Money   Too many vacations have been cut short because too much money was lost at the tables. Be sure that you bring this book along to increase your chances of winning, *and don't allow gaming losses to negate the other leisure aspects of your trip!*

Once You Arrive

◆   Upon arriving at your destination, your immediate attention to a few simple tasks will help insure your safety and enjoyment:

Verify, Verify, Verify!   Once you arrive at your chosen casino/

resort or hotel, contact the people that you spoke to prior to making reservations. Confirm rates and conditions, comp programs, reservations for shows and attractions, etc.

Charge All Expenses to Your Room or Rating Card Your final rating by the casino may provide more benefits than you anticipated, including the cost of shows, golf, tennis, spas, exercise facilities, and other recreational activities provided within the facility.

Each time that you begin a blackjack session, or change to another table, identify yourself as a player that is being rated.

Be Sure That You Receive the Compensations to Which You Are Entitled Talk to the casino host, casino marketing department, pit boss, or front desk personnel to insure that you receive the full benefits of the rating system.

Allow sufficient time on the last day of your trip to resolve any problems. I recently paid a $96 golf greens fee (for which I should have been "comped") because I had to catch an airplane and had no time to correct the error.

Take Advantage of Fun Books Discount coupon packages are often provided in package tours or by the gambling facility, offering many benefits which are unrelated to casino marketing comps. These booklets offer "two for one" specials, free gifts, gaming "match play" chips, and discounts on food, services, and recreational activities. Take advantage of these additional "freebies."

Inspect Your Lodging When You First Arrive Remember that you don't want to be on the twenty-first floor of the hotel if you are acrophobic; you don't want to be in a room adjacent to a noisy ice machine; the air conditioner shouldn't sound like a freight train every time the compressor cuts on; the accommodations should be clean and fully stocked. It's much easier for the hotel staff to relocate you if you have not used the room initially assigned to you.

Again, Anticipate the Unexpected!   Find out the location of the nearest doctor and pharmacy. Check the in-house telephone numbers for security personnel or other services that you might require.

Stash Your Cash!   Many facilities provide in-room safes or safety deposit boxes. Use them. Gambling and vacation centers, in spite of the slick promotions by public relations departments, are magnets for pickpockets, purse-snatchers, burglars, and other thieves who go to great lengths to relieve you of your cash and credit cards. Use the security measures provided to you, and watch where you travel, especially late at night.

Be Polite, and Be Complimentary   No matter what problem may arise, abrupt language and a negative disposition will not help solve it. Regardless of whom you are addressing, try to begin a complaint with, "I'm really pleased with your _____ (fill in the blank), but..."

Casino, lodging, and food service personnel will appreciate your compliments and be more helpful in eliminating your criticisms.

Before Leaving, Compliment Your Host   A kind word or two, and a simple "thank you," can be as effective as a big tip. If your stay at the facility was lousy in spite of your efforts, write a letter to the manager when you return home, and tell your friends!

Prepare in Advance for Your Departure   The last day of a gambling related vacation is often the most hectic. Pack your luggage the night before, pay hotel bills early if possible, account for jewelry and cash, and be ready to depart on time. I used to have a very nice diamond ring, until I left it on a hotel room night stand in Las Vegas!

The Best Places to Play Blackjack

◆   At the present time (mid-1996) there are over five hundred casinos in North America, located in thirty states, Canada, and the Bahamas, as well as gambling ships which depart from coastal states and ply their trade just outside of territorial waters.

There are many factors that help determine which casinos offer the best opportunities for players. The criterion for selection, in order of importance, is as follows:

Rules   Expert players generally agree that the best casinos play by the following rules:

1. One-deck tables; the fewer number of decks being used, the better for the player.

2. "Player-friendly" rules, such as dealer stands on soft 17, double-down on any two cards, split as many times as desired, table limits at least forty times the minimum bet, "surrender" allowed, etc.

Lots of Playing Space Available   Players should have the option to move to a different table with no delay in playing time. In general, the fewer players at a table, the better the advantage to the expert player. Although casinos may have many blackjack tables, they often only open new tables when playing conditions are very overcrowded. No player likes to wait for an opportunity to sit down at a table.

A Generous "Comp" Program   The best locations offer free or discounted lodging and meals for moderate-level gamblers. It shouldn't be necessary to be a "high roller" to receive reasonable compensation for your playing time.

Economically Priced Lodging and Food Services   Every player, regardless of his betting habits, should be comfortably and inexpensively housed and fed when he is not playing the game.

Free or Inexpensive Entertainment Should Be Readily Available Operating a resort/casino may be one of the most profitable businesses going. The costs of having the best entertainers in show business should be absorbed by the guys making the most profit!

A Great Geographical Location The glamour of Las Vegas, the beaches and the Boardwalk of Atlantic City, Gulf Coast attractions, and the incredible beauty of Lake Tahoe should be experienced by everyone, even those who don't like to gamble!

Easy Accessibility The average player should be able to get to the casino without it costing him an arm and a leg. Plenty of free parking should be available to drivers, and the facility should be easily accessible by plane, train, or bus.

◆   In truth, casino operators don't provide the favorable conditions listed above out of the kindness of their hearts. *Competition forces them to do so.* Consequently, the more casinos, the better the environment for the player.

Conversely, one of the largest and most heavily attended casinos in the United States, located in Connecticut, fails to provide many of the conditions favored by expert players, simply because it has a monopoly due to its geographical location.

Many of the great places to play blackjack are listed on the next few pages, and are presented in order of state, name, and city. Most have toll-free numbers which can be obtained by calling the "800" telephone operator. For a comprehensive list, contact the bookstores or publishers listed at the conclusion of this book.

In order for a casino to be included in the following list, it must offer the game of blackjack, and have at least five thousand square feet of gaming area, unless it's in a state that offers limited gaming opportunities.

When calling these establishments, determine the number of tables available, betting limits, the requirements of the comp program, costs of lodging and food, and other nongambling entertainment available.

National Casino Listings

California

Bicycle Club Casino (Bell Gardens)
Barona Casino (Lakeside)
Cache Creek Indian Casino (Brooks)
Casino Morongo (Cabazon)
Fantasy Springs Casino (Indio)
Robinson Rancherio Casino (Nice)
San Manuel Indian Casino (Highland)
Spotlight 29 Casino (Coachella)
Sycuan Gaming Center (El Cajon)
Table Mountain Rancheria Casino (Friant)
Viejas Valley Casino & Turf Club (Alpine)
Win-River Casino Bingo (Redding)

Colorado

$5 maximum bet blackjack is available in the mining towns of Black Hawk, Central City, and Cripple Creek. Contact the Chamber of Commerce in each town for a comprehensive listing of establishments.

Connecticut

Foxwoods Resort Casino (Ledyard)
The Mohegan Sun (Montville)

Florida

Land-based casinos and riverboats are currently illegal. These listings refer to cruise ships or gambling vessels that sail on day or evening "cruises to nowhere," outside of the territorial limits of the state.

Discovery I & II (Ft. Lauderdale and Miami)
Empress Cruise Line (Clearwater and St. Petersburg)
Europa SeaKruz (Key West, Ft. Myers Beach, and Maderia Beach)
Fernandina Cruise Lines (Fernandina Beach)
Hollywood Casino Cruises (Hollywood)
La Cruise (Atlantic Beach)
Sea Escape (Ft. Lauderdale)
SunCruz Casino (Key Largo, Ft. Lauderdale)
Tropicana Casino Cruises (Miami)
Vegas Express (Dania)

Georgia

Golden Isle Cruise Lines (Brunswick)

Illinois

Alton Belle Riverboat Casino (Alton)
Casino Queen (East St. Louis)
Empress Casino (Joliet)
The Grand Victoria Casino (Elgin)
Harrah's Joliet Casino, Harrah's Northern Star, Harrah's Southern Star (Joliet)
Jumer's Casino (Rock Island)
Par-A-Dice Riverboat Casino (East Peoria)
Players Casino (Metropolis)
Silver Eagle Casino (East Dubuque)

Iowa

Belle of Sioux City Casino (Sioux City)
Casino Omaha (Onawa)
Catfish Bend Riverboat (Fort Madison)
Dubuque Diamond Jo (Dubuque)
Lady Luck Casino (Bettendorf)
Meskwaki Casino (Tama)
Miss Marquette Riverboat Casino & Resort (Marquette)
Mississippi Belle II Riverboat Casino (Clinton)
The President Riverboat (Davenport)
Winna Vegas Casino (Sloan)

Louisiana

Belle of Baton Rouge (Baton Rouge)
Belle of Orleans, Bally's Casino Lakeshore Resort (New Orleans)
Boomtown Casino (Harvey)
Casino Rouge (Baton Rouge)
Cypress Bayou Casino (Charenton)
Flamingo Casino (New Orleans)
Grand Casino Avoyelles (Marksville)
Grand Casino Coushatta (Kinder)
Harrah's Shreveport Casino (Shreveport)
The Horseshoe Casino and Hotel (Bossier City)
Isle of Capri Casino (Bossier City)
Players Landing Casino (Lake Charles)
River City Casino (New Orleans)
Star Casino (Lake Charles)
Treasure Chest Casino (Kenner)

Michigan

Kewadin Shores Casino (St. Ignace)
Kings Club Casino (Brimley)
Lac Vieux Desert Casino (Watersmeet)

Leelanau Sands Casino (Suttons Bay)
Ojibwa Casino Resort (Baraga)
Soaring Eagles Card Room (Mt. Pleasant)
Vegas Kewadin Casino (Sault Ste. Marie)

Minnesota

Black Bear Casino (Carlton)
Firefly Creek Casino (Granite Falls)
Fond-du-Luth Casino (Duluth)
Fortune Bay Casino (Tower)
Grand Casino Hinckley (Hinckley)
Grand Casino Mille Lacs (Onamia)
Grand Portage Lodge and Casino (Grand Portage)
Jackpot Junction Casino (Morton)
Lake of the Woods Lodge and Casino (Warroad)
Mystic Lake Casino and Dakota Country Casino (Prior Lake)
Northern Lights Casino (Walker)
Palace Bingo and Casino (Cass Lake)
Red Lake Casino (Red Lake)
River Road Casino (Thief River Falls)
Shooting Star Casino (Mahnomen)
Treasure Island Casino (Welch)

Mississippi

Ameristar Casino (Vicksburg)
Bally's Saloon, Gambling Hall & Hotel (Tunica)
Bayou Caddy's Jubilee Casino (Lakeshore)
Biloxi Belle Casino and Resort (Biloxi)
Boomtown Casino (Biloxi)
Casino Magic—Bay St. Lewis (Bay St. Lewis)
Casino Magic Biloxi (Biloxi)
Circus Belle Casino (Robinsonville)
Copa Casino (Gulfport)

Cotton Club Casino (Greenville)
Fitzgerald's Casino (Robinsonville)
Grand Casino Biloxi (Biloxi)
Grand Casino Gulfport (Gulfport)
Harrah's Casino Hotel Vicksburg (Vicksburg)
Harrah's Casino Tunica (Robinsonville)
Hollywood Casino—Tunica (Robinsonville)
Isle of Capri Casino Crown Plaza Resort (Biloxi)
Isle of Capre Casino (Vicksburg)
Lady Luck Biloxi (Biloxi)
Lady Luck—Natchez (Natchez)
Lady Luck Rhythm and Blues Casino Hotel (Lula)
Palace Casino (Biloxi)
President Casino (Biloxi)
Rainbow Casino (Vicksburg)
Sam's Town Hotel and Gambling Hall (Robinsonville)
Sheraton Casino (Robinsonville)
Silver Star Hotel and Casino (Philadelphia)
Splash Casino (Tunica)
Treasure Bay Casino (Robinsonville)
Treasure Bay Casino Resort (Biloxi)

Missouri

Argosy Casino (Riverside)
Casino Aztar (Caruthersville)
Harrah's North Kansas City Casino (North Kansas City)
President Casino on the Admiral (St. Louis)
St. Charles Riverfront Station (St. Charles)
St. Jo Frontier Casino (St. Joseph)

Nevada

Due to the very large number of casinos available, only those with at least ten thousand square feet of gaming space are listed.

Las Vegas

Aladdin Hotel and Casino

Arizona Charlie's Inc.

Bally's Las Vegas

Barbary Coast Hotel and
Casino

Big Dog's Cafe and Casino

Binion's Horseshoe Club
Hotel and Casino

Boardwalk Hotel and Casino
Holiday Inn

Boulder Station Hotel and
Casino

Bourbon Street Hotel and
Casino

Buffalo Bill's Resort and
Casino

Caesars Palace

Circus-Circus Hotel and
Casino

Continental Hotel & Casino

Desert Inn Hotel

ElCortez Hotel and Casino

Ellis Island Casino

Eureka Casino

Excalibur Hotel and Casino

Flamingo Hilton Hotel and
Casino

Four Queens Hotel and
Casino

Frontier Hotel and Gambling
Hall

Gold Coast Hotel and Casino

Golden Nugget Hotel &
Casino

Hacienda Resort Hotel &
Casino

Hard Rock Hotel & Casino

Harrah's Casino Hotel

Hotel San Remo Casino &
Resort

Imperial Palace Hotel &
Casino

Jerry's Nugget

King 8 Hotel and Gambling
Hall

Lady Luck Casino Hotel

Las Vegas Club Hotel &
Casino

Las Vegas Hilton Hotel and
Casino

Luxor Hotel & Casino

Maxim Hotel & Casino

MGM Grand Hotel, Casino &
Theme Park

The Mirage

Monte Carlo Hotel & Casino

Nevada Palace Hotel &
Casino

New York, New York Casino
Resort

Palace Station Hotel & Casino

Poker Palace Casino

Port Tack Restaurant

Quality Inn and Casino

Rainbow Vegas Hotel & Casino
Rio Suite Hotel & Casino
Rivieria Hotel & Casino
Royal Hotel Casino
Sahara Hotel & Casino
Sam Boyd's California Hotel, Casino, and RV Park
Sam Boyd's Fremont Hotel and Casino
Sam's Town Hotel & Gambling Hall
Sands Hotel Casino
Santa Fe Hotel and Casino

Showboat Hotel & Casino
Silver City Casino
Stratosphere Hotel & Casino
Stardust Resort & Casino
Treasure Island at the Mirage
Treasure Island Hotel & Casino
Tropicana Resort & Casino
Union Plaza Hotel
Vacation Village Resort & Casino
Western Hotel & Casino
Westward Ho Hotel & Casino

Jackpot

Barton's Club 93
Cactus Pete's Resort Casino

Horse Shu Club

Lake Tahoe (State line)

Caesars Tahoe Resort
Harrah's Casino Hotel—Lake Tahoe
Harvey's Resort Hotel and Casino

Hyatt Regency Lake Tahoe Resort & Casino
Lake Tahoe Horizon Casino Resort
Lakeside Inn & Casino

Laughlin

Colorado Belle Hotel & Casino
Don Laughlin's Riverside Resort Hotel & Casino
Edgewater Hotel & Casino
Flamingo Hilton—Laughlin

Gold River Resort Hotel Casino
Golden Nugget—Laughlin
Harrah' Casino Hotel—Laughlin
Pioneer Hotel & Gambling Hall

Reno

Bob Cashell's Horseshoe Club
  & Casino
Bonanza Casino
Circus Circus Hotel &
  Casino—Reno
Clarion Hotel Casino
Comstock Hotel & Casino
Eldorado Hotel Casino
Fitzgerald's Casino & Hotel
Flamingo Hilton—Reno

Gold Dust West Casino
Harrah's Casino Hotel—Reno
Nevada Club Casino
Peppermill Hotel Casino
Pioneer Inn Casino
Reno Hilton Resort
Riverboat Hotel & Casino
Sands Regency Hotel
Starlite Bowl
Virginian Hotel & Casino.

Sparks

Baldini's Sports Casino
Giudici's B Street Gambling
  Hall

Plantation Station Gambling
  Hall
Treasure Club Casino
Western Village Inn & Casino.

Other Locations

Cactus Jack's Senator Club
  Casino (Carson City)
Carson Nugget Casino
  (Carson City)
Carson Valley Inn Hotel &
  Casino (Minden)
El Capitan Lodge & Casino
  (Hawthorne)
Eldorado Casino (Henderson)
Exchange Club of Beatty
  (Beatty)
Fallon Nugget (Fallon)

Primadonna Resort & Casino
  (Jean)
Railroad Pass Hotel & Casino
  (Henderson)
Red Lion Inn & Casino
  (Winnemucca)
Saddle West Hotel & Casino
  (Pahrump)
Si Redd's Casino (Mesquite)
Silver Smith Casino Resort
  (West Wendover)
Stockman's Bar, Restaurant, &
  Casino (Fallon)

Fourway Bar
  Cafe & Casino (Wells)
Gold Strike Hotel &
  Gambling Hall (Jean)
Gold Strike Inn & Casino
  (Boulder City)
Jax Casino (Lovelock)
Joe's Tavern (Hawthorne)
Joker's Wild (Henderson)
Lake Mead Lounge & Casino
  (Henderson)
Mac's Casino (West
  Wendover)

Owl Club Casino & Motel
  (Battle Mountain)
Stockmen's Motor Hotel &
  Casino (Elko)
Tahoe Biltmore Lodge &
  Casino (Crystal Bay)
Topaz Lodge & Casino (Topaz
  Lake)
Triple J Bingo Hall & Casino
  (Henderson)
Virgin River Hotel Casino &
  Bingo (Mesquite)
Whiskey Pete's Hotel &
  Casino (Jean)

New Jersey

All casinos are located in Atlantic City.

Bally's Park Place Casino
  Hotel & Tower
Caesars Atlantic City
Claridge Casino Hotel
Harrah's Casino Hotel
Merv Griffin's Resort Casino
  Hotel
Sands Hotel & Casino
Showboat Hotel & Casino

The Grand—A Bally's Casino
  Resort
Tropicana
Trump Plaza Hotel & Casino
Trump Taj Mahal Casino
  Resort
Trump World's Fair Casino
Trump's Castle Casino Resort

New Mexico

Camel Rock Casino (Santa Fe)
Casino Sandia (Albuquerque)
Inn of the Montana Gods Casino (Mescalero)
Isleta Gaming Palace Casino (Albuquerque)
Oh-Kay Casino & Bingo (San Juan Pueblo)

Pojoaque Gaming, Inc. (Santa Fe)
Santa Ana Star Casino (Bernalillo)
Sky City Tribal Casino (Acomita)

New York

Turning Stone Casino (Verona)

North Dakota

$5 maximum bet; $50 maximum bet at Indian casinos
Dakotha Sioux Casino (St. Michael)
Four Bears Casino & Lodge (New Town)
Prairie Knights Casino & Lodge (Fort Yates)
Super 8 Lounge (Williston)
Turtle Mountain Chippewa Casino (Belcourt)

South Dakota

This state limits players to a $5 maximum bet. Most casinos are located in Deadwood.

Washington

Lummi Casino (Bellingham)
Mill Bay Casino (Manson)
Muckleshoot Indian Casino (Auburn)
Nooksack River Casino (Deming)
Quileute Tribe Casino (LaPush)
Seven Cedars Casino (Saquim)
Swinomish Casino & Bingo (Anacortes)
Tulalip Bingo & Casino (Marysville)
Two Rivers Casino (Davenport)

Wisconsin

Bad River Bingo & Casino (Odanah)
Ho-Chunk Casino (Baraboo)

Hole-in-the-Wall Casino Hotel (Danbury)
Isle Vista Casino (Bayfield)
Lake of the Torches Casino (Lac du Flambeau)
LCO Casino (Hayward)
Menominee Casino Hotel & Bingo (Keshena)
Mohican North Star Casino (Bowler)
Mole Lake Casino (Crandon)
Oneida Bingo & Casino (Green Bay)
Potawatomi Bingo Casino (Milwaukee)
Rainbow Casino (Nekoosa)
St. Croix Casino & Hotel (Turtle Lake)

◆   When making your selection from the many casinos listed above, keep in mind that there is no such thing as a *bad* casino; some are just better than others!

By the Way...

If your travel costs are approximately the same, and you want to play blackjack in either Atlantic City or Las Vegas, which destination should you choose?

◆   In my opinion, Las Vegas is the hands-down winner—in terms of size alone.

Atlantic City currently has twelve casinos with a combined total of 794,173 square feet of space devoted to gambling.

The sixty-seven Las Vegas casinos listed in this book—those with at least 10,000 square feet of gambling space—have a combined total of 4,103,721 square feet of space devoted to gambling. This is the equivalent of sixty-six football fields!

Also, due to the competitive nature of Las Vegas, the costs of food, lodging, and entertainment are much lower than Atlantic City, and Las Vegas blackjack rules are more liberal.

◆   I've played blackjack in many casinos throughout the United States. I prefer to gamble in the following locations (listed alphabetically):

> Atlantic City—The Sands, Showboat.
> Biloxi—Casino Magic, Grand Casino.
> Colorado—Harvey's, Central City
> Florida—SeaEscape, Discovery, SunCruz.
> Gulfport—Grand Casino Gulfport.
> Las Vegas—Excalibur, Caesar's Palace, Monte Carlo, the Mirage, Tropicana.
> Lake Tahoe—Harvey's.
> Reno—Eldorado.

One more bit of information for those of you who are frequent visitors to casinos in Nevada. Call 602-636-1649, and order *Las Vegas Insider*. This monthly newsletter provides great information about the best gambling deals, the best food and lodging deals, the latest additions (or deletions) in casinos, and lots of gaming advice from its famous editor, Donald Currier. It's inexpensive, and it's fun to read!

Also, I believe that the best national guide to casino locations is published by *Casino Vacations* (P.O. Box 703, Dania, Florida 33004). Steve Bourie writes a comprehensive book, *American Casino Guide*, which is updated annually, that lists casino gambling establishments in thirty states—every casino/resort in the United States—plus Indian and riverboat casinos, too! This guide is moderately priced, and contains over $300 in casino comp coupons. Call *Casino Vacations* at 954-989-2766, if this publication is not available at your local bookstore.

Putting It All Together
OR
Blackjack My Way

"A man with a new idea is a crank until the idea succeeds."

—MARK TWAIN

◆ It's my opinion that playing this game successfully—winning much more often then you lose—requires a combination of many different elements.

The methodology presented below is the culmination of my thirty years of academic study and playing experience, and includes much of the information and advice presented in this book. It satisfies my personal temperament, is compatible with my financial capabilities, and allows me to enjoy the game while realizing an overall profit for my efforts.

Although many elements of this method of play are based on statistical probability and only require a good memory and understanding of rules and strategy, there are still many opportunities for the player to make judgmental and tactical decisions that can substantially effect the outcome of play. These decisions are made on the basis of the player's conservative or aggressive tendencies, and the available choices are explained as various situations occur.

The overall rationale for this method of play is twofold: to have fun and to win. I consider both of these factors essential to the game.

Seven key elements make up this playing methodology:

1. "Player Friendly" Rules.
2. Favorably Physical Playing Conditions.
3. Properly Applied Basic Strategy.
4. "Casual" Card Counting.
5. Use of the Proper Betting System.
6. Application of the Proper Playing Tactics.
7. Overall Money Management.

Following is a complete explanation of these elements:

Player-Friendly Rules

Blackjack rules established by the casino can cause the player's chances of winning to vary by as much as 10 percent, meaning that in the long run the player will lose 10 percent more hands when house rules are the most unfavorable, regardless of his playing skills.

Obviously, the player should pick a casino environment where the initial odds against him are as low as possible.

I'm not comfortable playing this game unless the following rules are in effect:

- Dealer *must stand* on a soft 17.
- Dealer has one exposed card.
- Dealer wins only the initial wager if he has blackjack.
- Player can double-down on any two cards.
- Player can split any pair, and is allowed to split at least three times.

- Player can double-down after any split.
- The maximum bet at the table is at least twenty times the minimum bet.

In some geographical areas players are only allowed to double-down on an initial point count of 9, 10, or 11. Your only choice is to accept this limitation or not play.

In general, if the above rules are not in effect, *don't play*. The built-in odds against you are unacceptable.

Favorable Physical Playing Conditions

◆　　The casino should be large enough to accommodate your action, and there should be enough open tables to allow players to move frequently without having to wait for a seat.

There should also be enough tables with betting limits within your selected level of play. If your normal initial bet is $5, there should be enough $5 minimum bet tables to allow you to move around with ease.

The casino should have a liberal comp program, since any free or reduced-price food or lodging is like cash in your pocket.

It's also best to play in a casino where the dealers are friendly and courteous. If casino personnel take the enjoyment out of playing, select another location, and write a letter to the casino manager when you get home!

Properly Applied Basic Strategy

◆　　As previously explained, basic strategy tells you the long-term probability of winning or losing hands when certain cards are held by the dealer and the player. In most cases the player must follow the rules religiously, but I feel that there is room for flexibility when certain situations occur.

Basic strategy recommends that the player either stand, hit, split, or double-down whenever he has an advantage over the house, regardless of how small the advantage may be, and regardless of the size of the wager. I disagree with this recommendation, and suggest the following method of play:

If my initial bet has increased to three times its original amount (which often happens when my progressive betting system is followed) I modify the application of basic strategy by not doubling or splitting hands, with the required doubling of the wager, when the following card combinations occur:

I Hold	Dealer Has	Do Not
9	5	Double
9	2	Double
10	A	Double
A/2, A/3	4	Double
4/4	5 or 6	Split
5/5	A	Double

I simply hit these hands, and don't risk doubling my bet.

With the exception of these nine circumstances, where the player's long-term advantage over the house is extremely minimal, I follow the basic strategy recommendations of the *majority opinions* stated in the Basic Strategy chapter of this book.

Casual Card Counting

◆   It is my opinion that sophisticated plus/minus counting systems are obsolete in today's casinos.

Multiple decks and deep cuts have essentially eliminated the effectiveness of counting cards. Unless the player finds himself in a single-deck game where at least 80 percent of the deck is exposed, the advantages of card counting don't justify the mental strain required, and counting offers no reliable advantage to the player.

On the other hand, it is relatively simple to count the number of face cards, fives, or aces that have been exposed, even in a multiple-deck game. When my casual count reveals that the remainder of the shoe is favorable to the player, I *increase my wager by one unit;* when the remainder of the shoe is unfavorable to the player, I *reduce my wager by one unit*, or leave it at its present level, even if the previous hand was a winner.

If the cards are so unfavorable that I lose three consecutive hands, I *leave the table*, and play elsewhere.

Use of the Proper Betting System

◆   I prefer a betting system that is a modification of several of the systems described in a previous chapter.

To explain my system of progressive betting, I consider a $5 bet to be *one unit.* I start playing with a two-unit bet ($10 per hand). If I win the first hand, I pull all of my winnings, and begin the next hand with my original two-unit bet. With each successive win, I increase my wager by *one unit.*

If my bet should reach a total of *ten units,* I let it ride until I lose, and then return to my original two-unit bet.

If I double-down or split, and win both hands, I consider this to be the equivalent of winning two consecutive hands, and adjust my bet accordingly. I don't change the bet if the hand is a "push."

I use this betting system for the following reasons:

1. Each time I win the first hand I play, my next wager is equal to my original bet, and my bankroll (the amount I started with) is back to its original amount. I am playing with my profits, and future winning hands are all profit. Many other systems require at least two consecutive winning hands before the original investment is removed from the betting box.

2. Consecutive losing hands only result in the loss of my minimum bet. Some systems suggest that you "double up to catch up."

3. I can never lose more than three consecutive hands at a table, because I leave the table before the fourth hand is dealt! In effect, I avoid those times when a dealer has a "hot shoe."

4. I allow my original bet to increase five-fold, and leave it at that level until I lose, which gives me the chance to take advantage of the dealer while he is consistently losing.

Other systems tell the player to reduce the wager to the minimum level after winning three hands in a row, thus eliminating the potential profit created by a "hot" player shoe.

The chances of winning a lot of money in a very short period of time are very possible with my system, whereas other systems have very low profit expectations. I consider the potential gain to be worth the risk, especially when my original bankroll is still intact.

Application of the Proper Playing Tactics

◆   I apply *all* of the table tactics suggested in a previous chapter of this book.

The overall purpose of these tactics is to *have you control the game, and not let the game control you.*

I'm an emotional person by nature, and have been easily distracted by the actions of the dealer and other players, as well as by the short-term fluctuations in the flow of the cards. The main idea is to stay focused on your two reasons for gambling— to enjoy yourself, and to win!

Practicing the previously suggested tactics will greatly improve your chances of accomplishing these two goals.

Overall Money Management

◆　　I follow the money management system previously described in this book.

In addition, because of my compulsive nature, I never establish a *credit line* with a casino. A credit line allows the player to play with casino chips (often without an initial cash deposit), and pay with a personal check if he experiences losses at the conclusion of his gambling trip.

On the other hand, I always ask to be rated as a "cash player," and receive the same comps as a player with a credit line.

I've also learned to leave my credit cards at home! It's too easy to abandon money management principles "in the heat of battle," so don't risk temptation by having easy access to cash through your credit cards. Losing is bad enough, but getting the bill in the mail a month later is even worse!

◆　　The seven elements of play outlined in this chapter describe my current method of playing blackjack, based on my thirty years of playing experience and academic study of the game. My personality and personal motivations for playing are reflected in my method of play, and may not coincide with your temperament or personal goals.

In spite of this possibility, most of the suggestions presented are also recommended by other leading experts and writers in this field. If you disagree with the recommendations, ignore them, and do what you want to do! After all, it's your money, and you have the right to spend it any way you choose.

I read and *study* every new book or article about blackjack that I can get my hands on, and have modified my play over the years in order to apply my improved understanding of the game. You should do the same!

Potpourri

"A little of what you fancy does you good."
—MARIE LLOYD

This chapter contains the "odds and ends" that every author wants to include in his book, but can't find an appropriate place to put it. It may contain the most important information or it may be of no interest to you at all!

Blackjack Fever

◆   *Blackjack fever* is a common physiological virus that only attacks people who play the game of 21. It strikes without warning and its effects on a player can be devastating.

Symptoms of this virus include rapid heart beat and respiration, high blood pressure, profuse sweating, tension headaches, and intense physical agitation.

The psychological effects are often less obvious, but are more harmful than the physical reactions: irrational playing and betting decisions, radical mood swings from euphoric bliss to deep depression, anger directed at casino personnel and other players, self-pity, and a sense of either complete invincibility or total defeat.

An attack of blackjack fever occurs without warning, and can last for only a few moments or for a lifetime, depending on the vulnerability of the victim.

It can attack a player at the top of a winning streak as well as a player who is losing consistently.

The overall effect of the fever is that he will have a miserable time and lose a lot of money!

Fortunately this disease is not terminal, and once a player recognizes the symptoms, steps can be taken to alleviate its effects on his play:

1. Drink plenty of *nonalcoholic* liquids.

2. Eat healthy foods; leave the tables and go to the buffet or snack bar.

3. Get lots of sleep; go to your room and go to bed!

If you plan to stay in the casino in spite of your fevered condition, the following suggestions are recommended:

1. *Think* about what you are doing. Don't allow yourself to deviate from your normal masterful playing and money management strategies.

2. Take a short break from the game, go to the rest room, and splash cold water on your face!

3. Make every effort to regain control of your emotions; calm down!

Once you are away from the casino environment, the symptoms of blackjack fever dissipate quickly. If you suffer recurrent attacks of the fever every time you play blackjack, switch to another casino game or learn to play golf!

My Personal Blackjack Experience

◆ My experience as a blackjack player has been long and evolutionary.

My mother taught me the rules of the game when I was eleven years old. She is still an avid blackjack player at the age of seventy-eight, and travels to Biloxi and Gulfport from her home in Sarasota, Florida, at least three times a year, and joins me occasionally on the gambling ships that sail out of Ft. Lauderdale. She's a great player and money manager, and seldom loses.

I played blackjack in smoky dormitory rooms in college, changing dealers (and the bank) whenever a blackjack was dealt. These long, low-stakes games were enjoyable, but played havoc with my grade-point average on several occasions.

My first casino experience occurred in 1969, when I was twenty-five years old. Friends in the local civic club invited me on a "minijunket" to the El Casino Resort (now the Princess Resort and Casino) on Grand Bahama Island, proclaimed to be the largest casino in North America at the time.

I was immediately fascinated by the glitz and glamour of the facility, and although I knew little about basic strategy or money management, I remember winning ten hands in a row (at a bet of $5 per hand) and ended up $80 ahead for the trip. I decided that this game was easy to win at, and shortly thereafter purchased Dr. Thorp's, *Beat The Dealer*, in order to sharpen my skills.

I returned to Freeport and the El Casino on many occasions, and also played at Paradise Island in Nassau.

I continued to like the atmosphere of the casinos, but discovered that my original good luck was not a regular occurrence. In fact, I lost eight out of ten times that I played! I took advantage of the free alcoholic beverages being served, wagered spontaneously, and tried to "outguess" the cards.

My first experience in Las Vegas was an eye-opener. The Bahamas paled in comparison to the newly-opened MGM Grand Casino (the *original* MGM Grand), which I visited with three "high roller" friends.

Due to their credit ratings, we were treated like kings—free rooms, first-class dining, the works! I started gambling with a bankroll of $1,200 intended to last for three days, and lost $1,100 playing blackjack in the first three hours!

I'm a decent poker player, and switched from blackjack to the seven-card stud games. After playing for several hours, I took my winnings of $155, and returned to the blackjack tables—and promptly lost it! This pattern continued for the next three days (winning at poker and losing at blackjack), and I returned to Fort Lauderdale with $28 in cash in my wallet. I had missed most meals, had slept a total of four hours during my four-day/three-night stay in Las Vegas, and experienced the worst case of "blackjack fever" that I've ever had.

In spite of my losing track record, I still enjoyed playing the game, and rationalized my poor playing habits as being a simple case of bad luck. I continued to purchase books for my personal blackjack library, read them with interest, and ignored the advice from the experts without realizing that I was doing so!

Even though my home state of Florida didn't allow casino gambling in the 1980s, gambling ships became popular on the Southeast coast, and I became (and still am) a regular customer on these "cruises to nowhere."

Cruise ships and other smaller vessels are allowed to go beyond territorial waters (in this case, three miles) and conduct full casino gambling in international waters. After one prolonged series of losses, intermingled with an occasional winning night, I realized that it might be smart to rethink my game plan.

After rereading several of the better books about how to play blackjack, it finally occurred to me that I wasn't playing by the proper rules! A friend compared my playing habits to that of a golfer who always shoots in the high 90s (a lousy score, for you nongolfers) in spite of his efforts, because he never learned the proper "basic swing" and the other fundamentals required to play the game successfully.

As time passed, my playing skills improved, and—low and behold!—my losses declined and my winning sessions increased!

In other words, I stopped being a typical blackjack player and became a knowledgeable one.

In 1990 my wife and our seven-year-old son vacationed in Las Vegas. Even though she is a "reluctant" gambler (hates to lose!) she shares my enjoyment of the casinos and the other excellent entertainment available. We own our own business, and manage to take two to three weeklong vacations per year, several of which have been spent in the gambling meccas of North America. My son is positive that the best video arcades and the latest games are in Las Vegas, Reno, Lake Tahoe, and Atlantic City!

Four years ago (1992), my wife and I decided to co-author a travel book designed for those who enjoy gambling, and are interested in the many nongaming activities provided by gambling establishments. This book, *A Family Guide to Gambling in the U.S.A.*, was published in early 1994.

In early 1995 I wrote and published a booklet entitled *Blackjack—35 Tips to Make You a Winner!!*, a twenty-eight page primer that will help the novice player to learn the most important aspects of the game in an hour, and presents a conservative approach to basic strategy and money management that should prevent him from being wiped out on his first visit to a blackjack table.

At this point in my gaming experience, I consider myself well-versed in the game. I practice what I preach, and I win more often than I lose. I will continue to play the game as long as my physical and mental abilities allow me to do so, not to mention the required bankroll!

What Do Casino Employees Think of Players

◆   In 1995 I wrote a magazine article that attempted to explain how dealers and pit bosses feel about the customers that they face across the tables.

This article is based on casual as well as formal interviews with blackjack dealers and pit bosses in Las Vegas, Lake Tahoe, Reno, Atlantic City, and Florida. It presents what I believe is a candid and factual picture of what casino personnel think of blackjack players, and should provide some helpful hints as to how you should conduct yourself while playing this game.

BLACKJACK—OBSERVATIONS FROM THE OTHER SIDE OF THE TABLE

You're a blackjack player, or you wouldn't be reading this article. So am I, and many times we've sat eyeball to eyeball across a half-round table facing Him. He deals the cards—that model of aloof superiority in the crisp white shirt and black bow tie—*the Dealer!*

Occasionally this person is our friend, well deserving of our tips, praise, and applause as we match wits, skill, and luck, and come out on top as a winner! Most other times he seems like the "Piranha of the Casino," eating our chips like colorful snack foods while we moan and groan with disbelief, "Doesn't this guy ever lose?" or "Every time the cards are going my way, they change dealers!" or "That dealer was so fast, I lost my count on the cards!" and so on, and so on...

Yes, that's what we think of the dealers, but what do they think of us? Our playing skills? Our attitude? Our behavior? And what about the Pit Boss, who lurks like a vulture, eyeing our every move, waiting to feed on the remnants in our purses and wallets? What is his opinion of us? *This is your chance to find out!*

In order to answer these age-old questions, and to satisfy my insatiable thirst for knowledge, I convinced about a dozen pit bosses and dealers from various casinos around the country to answer a series of prepared questions that would allow them to bare their souls and tell us what they truly feel about blackjack players. The identities and places of employment of the respondents are strictly confidential, since they refused to participate if they might be subject to the wrath of their employers and customers if their names were revealed!

Keep in mind that these are the thoughts, impressions, and opinions of the guys and gals "in the trenches," the dealers and pit bosses—not those of the casino executives, marketing directors, or public relations managers.

Similar questions were asked to both dealers and pit bosses, often in casual, across-the-table conversation, but in most cases in actual interview situations that were conducted away from the casino floor. Their responses were so similar that they are often combined to insure brevity in this article.

The most pertinent questions, and a compilation of the responses, are as follows:

QUESTION: "What are your responsibilities as a dealer?"

RESPONSE: (Dealer) "To be sure that the cards are properly shuffled and dealt to the players, bets are correctly wagered, and losing or winning hands are collected or paid. I'm also expected to watch for players who might be cheaters (grifters), expert card counters, or those who are potentially disruptive due to drugs or alcohol—people who don't play by the rules or could 'cause a scene' at my table."

RESPONSE: (Pit Boss) "To supervise the mechanics of the game, account for all cash received and chips dispersed at each table, settle disputes between players and dealers, verify the honesty and integrity of the players and the dealer, and, when necessary, alter table conditions to improve the chances of a profitable session for my employer (the casino).

QUESTION: "What do you mean, 'alter table conditions'?"

RESPONSE: "There are many ways that we can attempt to break a winning streak by one player, or convince an unruly player to leave our assigned area of responsibility—such as changing dealers, shuffling the decks more often, slowing down or speeding up the deal, distracting the player with idle conversation, increasing the minimum bet requirements, and other ways. It's sometimes necessary to slow down a "hot" player, or one who is too drunk or disruptive to be playing in the first place!

QUESTION: "You mentioned 'card counters'—do they really hurt the house?"

RESPONSE: "Not really, since six-deck shoes and shallow cuts pretty well eliminate the advantages of card counting, and most counters aren't accurate enough in their count to make a real difference. Most players don't even understand the basic rules of the game!

QUESTION: "What are the most common mistakes made by black-jack players?"

RESPONSE: "There are so many of them! But here are a few: Lack of knowledge of the game; not following the easily learned strategies needed to play successfully. Even seasoned players often ignore the odds and don't split or double-down or hit or stand when they should."

"Poor money management; having no system of increasing or decreasing their bets, and betting based on 'hunches,' anger, greed, or alcohol!"

"Playing blackjack when they are too tired to concentrate, are madat their wife (husband), lost too much the day before and are trying to 'catch up,' and any number of other things which distract them from concentrating on the game."

"Not knowing when to quit. I've often seen players win big, and then lose it all back and a lot more, because they expected too much from a single session of play."

"Strangely enough, many wealthy people think it's fun to lose large sums of money in front of their friends and family; we don't understand the rationale, but it's a fairly common thing to witness."

"Most players don't understand the game, don't concentrate on what they're doing, don't listen to advise offered by knowledgeable players, and blame us for their losses. It's players like these that pay our salaries and help us build new casinos!"

QUESTION: "Do 'hot' and 'cold' tables really exist?"

RESPONSE: "Absolutely, as do hot and cold players. In a short period of time, the worst player can win every hand and the expert player can lose every hand."

QUESTION: "What's the most stupid question you've ever been asked by a player?"

RESPONSE: [The responses were numerous and humorous. These are my favorites.]

[Directed to a cruise ship pit boss] "What time is the Midnight Buffet?"

[Directed to a dealer whose table was next to a staircase.] "How do I get upstairs?"

[Directed to a pit boss that was on a cruise ship on a twenty-seven-day cruise.] "Do you stay here on the ship?" [Her response, "No, they fly me in by helicopter each morning, just for you players!"]

[Question directed to *many* dealers.] "Do I have to make a bet before I see my cards?"

[Directed to a dealer after the player had lost over $800 in less than ten minutes.] "Do I have to get 21 every time to win?"

QUESTION: "If you had to make a living as a blackjack player, how would you go about it?"

RESPONSE: "First, I don't think I could; the house advantages are too great. But if I had to…

"I'd learn to play the game properly. I'd read the books and follow the recommendations of the experts, rely on the long-term odds, and manage my money carefully."

"I'd take advantage of the casino whenever possible. I'd take any comps available, and ask for them if they weren't offered. I'd cut my overhead expenses with every 'freebie' I could get."

"I would take advantage of poorly trained dealers or pit bosses. Not all dealers are experts at their job; many make common mistakes that might reveal the value of their hole card, like "flashing" the card to a player unintentionally, or by looking at a hole card more than once to be sure it isn't an ace, or by paying a hand that should have been a 'push' or a loser."

"I'd only tip the dealer if he was helping me be a winner; a toke for a lousy dealer is a bad investment."

"I would treat the dealer *as I like to be treated*." I would be cordial and polite, not blame him for my losses, tip him if I was winning, and thank him for his efforts. If his actions as a dealer or a pit boss annoyed me in any way, I'd leave the table and find another place to play."

"I would know when to quit. I would set reasonable limits on how much I hoped to win and how much I could afford to lose during a session of play."

So, this is what the "hired help" told me about what they think of us. The next time you take your chances at the game of 21, remember that dealers and pit bosses are people, too. How you treat them may have a substantial effect on your financial success. Good Luck!!

Conversations Overheard at the Blackjack Table

◆ "I almost broke the bank last night, until..."

"The dealer had a 6 showing, so I split my eights and doubled-down on both hands. Would you believe the dealer drew five cards to 21?"

"I *never* hit a 15 or 16; I'll let the dealer bust."

"The way they give money away around here, I don't know how this place stays in business!"

""But, honey—I'm way ahead! We can't leave now!"

"I don't care if it's been two days—When I get hungry I'll stop playing and get something to eat."

"Why did you hit your 12 when the dealer had a 2 showing? Don't you know how to play this game?"

"Just give me two more hours. I know I can win it all back!"

"Doesn't this dealer ever bust?"

"Will you hold me seat while I go get some more money?"

"My chart says you're not supposed to hit that hand!"

"We flew in yesterday, but I haven't seen our room yet. My wife says it's nice!"

Gambling and the I.R.S.

The Internal Revenue Service has a number of general rules that explain how the taxpayer should report his winnings and losses.

Those relating to casino blackjack players in 1996 are presented below:

1. Claim all winnings (1010.02.B.9.e).

2. Claim the fair market value of all complimentary gifts, including goods, merchandise, entertainment, lodging, meals, and services (1320.03.A).

3. The establishment (the payor) is required to withhold 28 percent of the gross amount of winnings less the amount of the wagers, provided the net winnings are more than $5000, or where the proceeds are least 300 times as large as the wager (1320.07.A).

4. A taxpayer who pursues gambling activities full-time, with regularity, and as his livelihood, is engaged in a trade or business, even though he is not holding himself out to the public as a supplier of goods or services (2110.01.c.1.d). If the ordinary and necessary test and the carrying on test are met, losses are deductible trade or business expenses.

5. The occasional gambler is *not* to deduct losses like a professional, but can deduct his losses as an itemized deduction up to the amount of his winnings (2350.03.E). Gambling income is reported on the taxpayer's Form 1040, but the losses must be reported as an itemized deduction on Schedule A.

6. Gambling winnings exempts from tax a nonresident alien's gambling winnings from table games of chance (7120.03.B.12).

7. To report gambling winnings, request Form W-2G, Certain Gambling Winnings, from the Internal Revenue Service.

One Day at Foxwoods

◆   My wife, twelve-year-old son, and I visited this tribal casino in Ledyard, Connecticut, in mid-August, 1995. We arrived in the early afternoon on a Tuesday, spent the night, and departed for a New England vacation the next morning.

This establishment is huge, and first class in every respect. We stayed in the Two Trees Inn, adjacent to the casino, which is one of the two lodging options available to patrons. The room had the special amenities that you find in better quality hotels, and the staff was courteous and friendly.

The casino and entertainment complex is housed in a gigantic building about five-hundred yards from the inn, and is comparable to the better strip casinos in Las Vegas. We entered the facility in mid-afternoon and toured the entire complex, which contains several restaurants, two spacious casinos, a large bingo area, shopping arcades, turbo-motion theaters (my favorite is Dino Island!), a cinedrome theater, video arcade, big-name showroom, and much more!

I obtained my own "Wampum Club" card, so that my play could be rated for comps, and began playing blackjack about 7:00 P.M. I started with an $800 bankroll, and played two hands on each deal with an initial unit bet of $10 per hand.

Rules of play are very similar to the strip in Las Vegas, except that pairs can only be split one time. Maximum allowable bets were at least twenty times the minimum table limit, which were unusually high. I only saw one $5 table and only about a dozen $10 tables; the rest, dozens of them, had $15 to $50 minimums.

I lost for the first hour of play, and moved frequently, presenting my rating card to the pit boss each time I sat at a different table.

My wife played for a while, but soon quit because she didn't like the high minimum bet required.

At 8:30 P.M., I called a pit boss over and explained that I had only been playing for a short period of time, but would be playing after dinner, and asked if he could comp my family at the buffet. He said he would check, and came back a few minutes later with three complimentary buffet tickets. He said that I hadn't been playing long enough to be rated, but gave us the free meals anyway, proving that it never hurts to ask!

We went to dinner, and I returned to the tables at 10:00 P.M. I had to play at the $25 minimum tables, because all of the lower minimum tables were full, with players waiting.

At 11:15 P.M. I was a $700 loser, and once again moved to another table. I played for forty-five minutes, had three very favorable shoes, and won back $850. I tipped the dealer $10, and quit for the night, $140 ahead.

The next morning, I was informed that I had earned $31 in comp money, which paid for our breakfast and allowed a discount on our room cost. I played blackjack for ten minutes, won $50, and checked out of the hotel to continue our vacation. Our total expenses were $151, and my winnings totaled $190. In effect, three people spent the night in a very nice hotel, had dinner and breakfast, and the establishment gave us $39 in profit! I wish it happened like this all the time!

Even though we had a great time at Foxwoods, I can't recommend this casino for the serious player, due to the high table minimums and the overcrowded conditions which prevent easy movement from table to table.

Indian Gaming

A major growth in casino gambling has occurred in the last few years as a result of the establishment of casinos on Indian reservations. Over one hundred casino-style gambling facilities have opened, the vast majority being located in states that previously disallowed casino gambling.

This growth has occurred because of federal law (Indian Gaming Regulatory Act, 1988) which permits casino games in those states that allow them, even if they are only allowed for charity groups.

In most cases, the tribe must form a "compact" with the state, which shares in the profits. Other state governments have fought against tribal gambling operations, and the tribes operate their casinos without state approval.

Many of the Indian casinos are small concerns, offering a few table games, bingo, and pull-tab slot machines. Others, such as Foxwoods and the Mohegan Sun (Connecticut) and Mystic Lake and the Grand (Minnesota), are among the largest casinos in the world!

The primary beneficiaries of Indian gaming are the tribes themselves, allowing many of them a self-sufficiency never before experienced. Although Indian gaming only represents about 7 percent of national gaming revenues, the profits from casino operations are spent by the tribes in the local communities, resulting in 250,000 direct or indirect jobs, 85 percent of which are held by non-Indians. Dozens of health clinics, fire departments, and government and public service facilities and activities are being provided to tribal members without use of federal, state, or local taxes.

As of 1995, ninety-five tribes are benefiting from gaming revenues in excess of $6 billion, and providing casino gaming to many local residents who can't afford the time or money to travel to the major gambling centers.

Many state governments continue attempting to dislodge or tax these Indian casinos in spite of their benefits to the tribes and local communities, and their popularity among many local residents.

◆   In my opinion, it's time for the federal government, and the federal court system, to clarify its position on Indian gaming. The tribal nations should be allowed to conduct business without harassment from state and local politicians.

Luck—Does It Affect Your Game?

◆   Do I always win at blackjack? Of course not! In fact, I often have losing sessions, sometimes four or five in a row!

Many writers tell you that luck has no part in the game; I think that luck plays a *major* part in the short-term outcome of play.

At this point in your reading, you should be convinced that I have a fairly decent understanding of blackjack, and know how to competitively play the game. But, bastardizing a famous quote, "Blackjack is a game that can try men's souls." After many years of casino gambling, and hundreds of thousands of hands, I believe that I have experienced the best and the worst luck possible!

Ken Uston, author of *Million Dollar Blackjack*, organized teams of expert players who used card counting and basic strategy skills to win at single-deck games prior to the time that casinos altered rules to offset the advantage to the players. In spite of his success, he cites many occasions when his teams lost thousands of dollars over extended periods of time.

I attribute these losses to bad luck, whereas other writers claim that the casinos were cheating the players, or that these losing sessions are only short-term "fluctuations" in the flow of the cards.

Still other writers advise you to *decrease* your bet if you win several hands in a row, thus reducing your potential winnings if good luck should occur!

I believe that if you play the game "by the book," you will still experience periods of good and bad luck.

Several years ago I was on a "turnaround" junket to the Princess Casino in Freeport, Grand Bahama Island. The flight left Fort Lauderdale at 7:45 P.M., and returned at 1:45 A.M., allowing about five hours of time at the tables. I began play about 8:30 P.M. (it's only a twenty-two-minute flight from Florida to the Bahamas!). I spent the entire evening in the same chair at the same table, never had a losing shoe (meaning that I won money on every six-deck shoe that was dealt), and left the casino in time to make my 1:30 A.M. departure flight with a $3,700 profit in my wallet. Was this good luck, or skillful play?

Last year I was on one of the gambling ships departing from Fort Lauderdale for their regular five-hour evening cruise. I lost consistently for the entire trip. I never had a winning shoe, and changed tables at least twenty times, in keeping with my playing tactics explained in a previous chapter. Frankly, I'm embarrassed to tell you how much I lost that night! Was this bad luck, or am I a lousy blackjack player?

My daughter, a novice player, and I went out on this same ship last month. She won over $1,000 by following my advice, having started with $10 bets and a $100 bankroll. I lost $260 that night. Did luck have anything to do with these results?

Several months ago I was on a different gambling ship that departs from Fort Lauderdale. Near the end of the five-hour cruise, I was down $2,700, and won $3,600 in the last thirty minutes of playing time. Was this unskillful play followed by expert play, or was this bad luck followed by unusually good luck? Were the dealers cheating me, and then decided to give me back my losses, plus a profit, as a magnanimous gesture? I think not!

No matter what the other guys say, and no matter what your friends tell you, *luck, both good and bad,* can have a *major* effect on the short-term outcomes of play.

Cruise Ship Blackjack

◆   If you're planning to take a vacation cruise to such destinations as the Caribbean, Mexico, or Puerto Rico, and plan to play blackjack in the ship's casino, a bit of research could save you a lot of money!

Some cruise lines, such as Royal Caribbean and Carnival at the present time, advertise and practice "Las Vegas Rules" in their casinos, while others play by rules that seriously limit winning opportunities for their guests. By establishing rules that strongly favor the house, the unsuspecting cruise passenger can be facing a considerable disadvantage.

The most common restrictive rules are:

1. Dealer hits soft 17.
2. Player can only double-down on 10 or 11.
3. Player cannot resplit pairs.
4. An eight-deck shoe is used.
5. Table betting limits are very restricted.

These rules can add at least 5 percent to the normal house advantage.

In order to avoid having to play with unfavorable conditions, ask your travel agent for the telephone number of the casino manager on the ship, call him, and find out what games rules are offered. If you don't like the rules, let him know that you will be choosing another cruise line, and tell your travel agent to make a different selection. Eventually, better playing conditions will be available to cruise line passengers.

Compulsive Gambling

"Gambling Problem? Call 1-800-GAMBLER."

This statement, voluntarily included in many casino advertisements, is a result of the good work being done by the National Council on Problem Gambling and its twenty-seven state affiliates.

Founded in 1972, the National Council is a voluntary nonprofit organization whose primary purpose is to disseminate information and education on compulsive gambling as an illness and public health problem.

Their studies indicate that compulsive gambling is on the increase in the United States. A 1976 survey indicated a prevalence rate of between 7 and 8 percent, or 1.1 million "probable compulsive gamblers," whereas studies in 1995 showed rates of 7 percent in Louisiana and 5.4 percent in Iowa, indicating that states with more legalized gambling have more problems with problem or pathological gamblers.

In spite of these findings, the national organization takes a *neutral* stand on the issue of legalized gambling, while seeking to assist those citizens who are adversely affected as a result.

Who is a compulsive gambler? The Council defines compulsive gambling as "a progressive behavior disorder in which an individual has a psychologically uncontrollable preoccupation and urge to gamble. This results in excessive gambling, the outcome of which is the loss of time and money. The gambling reaches the point at which it compromises, disrupts, or destroys the gambler's personal life, family relationships, or vocational pursuits. These problems in turn lead to intensification of the gambling behavior. The cardinal features are emotional dependence on gambling, loss of control, and interference with normal functioning."

The American Psychiatric Association has established diagnostic criteria for identifying pathological gamblers:

A. Persistent and recurrent maladaptive gambling behavior as indicated by five or more of the following:

1. is preoccupied with gambling (e.g., preoccupied with reliving past gambling experiences, handicapping or planning the next venture, or thinking of ways to get money with which to gamble)

2. needs to gamble with increasing amounts of money in order to achieve the desired excitement

3. has repeated unsuccessful efforts to control, cut back, or stop gambling

4. is restless or irritable when attempting to cut down or stop gambling

5. gambles as a way of escaping from problems or of relieving a dysporic mood

6. after losing money gambling, often returns another day to get even ("chasing" one's losses)

7. lies to family members, therapist, or others to conceal the extent of involvement with gambling

8. has committed illegal acts such as forgery, fraud, theft, or embezzlement to finance gambling

9. has jeopardized or lost a significant relationship, job, or educational or career opportunity because of gambling

10. relies on others to provide money to relieve a desperate financial situation caused by gambling

B.   The gambling behavior is not better accounted for by a Manic Episode.

Demographically, males, nonwhites, younger individuals, and those with lower formal education appear to be at greater risk of developing gambling problems.

While there are over 13,000 programs for alcohol and other substance abuse problems throughout the United States, there are only about 100 treatment programs for pathological gamblers, none of which receive direct federal funding.

If you feel that you are a compulsive gambler, or are leaning in that direction, call the National Helpline (1-800-522-4700) for no obligation information and assistance.

Long-Term Versus Short-Term Play—Is There a Major Difference?

As a long-term player, I've struggled with the short-term fluctuations of casino gambling. This chapter attempts to provide solutions to this age old problem.

Anyone that has ever read books about casino gambling knows that there are three basic steps to becoming a winning player at any game offered:

1. The player must learn the rules of the game.
2. The player must learn the correct strategy required to improve his chances of winning.
3. The player must learn how to manage his money so that he can last through periods of losing and be able to take advantage of periods of winning.

This chapter relates to the second step in this process—learning the basic strategy for successful play at any casino game, and your faith in the recommendations made by the experts.

Specifically, this chapter examines the best strategies, and how these strategies will increase your potential to win and/or decrease your potential to lose. Which playing decisions will increase the amount won or decrease the amount lost over a period of time, and how do experts determine which playing decisions are correct?

The answer to this question is: computer analysis. Prior to the invention of high-speed computers, mathematical analysis of games of chance was laborious and time-consuming. The mathematical Theory of Probability, formulated by the French philosopher and mathematician Blaise Pascal (1623–1662), provided interested researchers with a method of predicting the roll of the dice and the flow of the cards. Gambling experts wrote their books and instructed their readers based on their personal experiences, or on the basis of a limited number of "trial runs"—simulated play of the cards, dice, wheel, or machine—where the results of each decision had to be manually identified and recorded. The computer, with its ability to perform microsecond calculations, totally revolutionized how gaming experts made their decisions about how to gamble in a casino.

During the last thirty years, writers like Thorp, Wong, Braun, Griffin, and others took casino games off the casino floor and developed computer programs that allowed them to play millions, even *billions* of rounds of play within a short period of time. They were able to determine the *best ways* to play each casino game, based on the *long-term results of simulated play. Simply stated, it's math and machines!* Computer programs are now available for use on your home computer that allow you to duplicate research that used to take years within the amount of time it would take you to prepare and eat a good meal!

All types of casino gaming have been analyzed by the experts. For instance, in the casino game of blackjack, the most *analyzed* game ever played, the computer told the experts that a player should double down on a hard count of 11, and that he should always hit a hard count of 16 if the dealer's exposed card is 7 or higher. In the first case, the player is likely to win more, and in the second case the player is likely to lose less *in the long run*. With video poker, the rules applied during the play of the table game are quite different than those suggested by the experts who write about the electronic version of this game. Analyses of many other forms of casino gambling, based on computer simulation, also present variations in play that often seem unacceptable to the average player.

The essential key to all reputable advice currently being offered by today's gaming experts—men and women who want you to purchase their books and profit from their recommendations—is *long-term expectation.*

So what does this mean to the average recreational gambler? What does this mean to you? I'll use my personal experience to attempt to answer this question.

I began gambling in casinos in 1970, with a two-day trip to El Casino (now the Bahamas Princess) in Freeport, Grand Bahama Island. I lost money playing most of the casino games, including blackjack. After returning to Fort Lauderdale, I purchased a book or two, and started learning how the games *should* be played. My first trip to Las Vegas was to the *original* MGM Grand, and I've been to most every other major casino vacation destination since then, including Lake Tahoe, Reno, Colorado, Louisiana, Mississippi, Atlantic City, the Bahamas, major cruise ships, and casino ships departing from various ports of call in Florida.

My principal game of choice has always been blackjack. Over the years I've improved my knowledge and skill at playing this game. I know basic strategy, can count cards when table conditions make it beneficial to do so, and consider myself to be an expert player. I've even written a book or two on the subject!

For the last ten years, I've played casino blackjack at least once every three to four weeks, averaging five to ten hours of play at each session. Combined with my earlier experience, I estimate that I've spent about two-thousand hours playing blackjack in a casino. I almost always play two hands, and probably average at least 120 hands per hour of play. Based on these rough estimates, I've played about 240,000 hands of blackjack in the last twenty-five years.

Does this mean that I've played enough to experience the overall long-term expectations of play? The answer is Maybe yes, and maybe no!

The strategies recommended by most blackjack gaming experts are based on at least nine million simulated hands of play. Many have extended their recommendations based on hundreds of millions of hands of play. In order to be 99 percent assured that my basic strategy play would reduce this game to almost even odds (no advantage to the house or the player), I would have to play *perfect strategy* for a total of 750,000 hours of play, averaging 120 hands per hour, to complete a nine-million hand simulation. If I began playing now, right this minute, it would take me about *one hundred and seventy* years of nonstop play to be 99 percent sure that the strategies recommended by the experts would result in the outcome that they predict!

On the other hand, some experts don't feel that a person must play *forever* to experience the predictable long-term results. Perhaps a sampling of 100,000 hands is sufficient for players to reap the benefits of following the basic strategy guidelines recommended by the experts.

Other variables also affect the reliability of long-term strategy, but aren't often clearly explained by writers of casino gaming books.

A major factor that seriously affects player outcome is the *volatility* of most casino games. Even though the experts tell us that we should win (or lose) X number of dollars after placing X number of bets over a long period of time, the amounts won or lost over a *short* period of time can and often do fluctuate dramatically. The numbers and the amounts vary, depending on the game. For example, assume that a game has a long-term expectation of plus $1 for every one hundred hands played, and assume that this predicted win rate is based on thousands and thousands of one-hundred-hand sessions. If you were to randomly select any one of these sessions, and examine the actual outcome of play, the actual cash won or lost would most likely be *dozens of times* greater or less than $1.

From personal experience I know that it is possible to sit down at a blackjack table and win every hand dealt from a six-deck shoe, or make eleven straight passes on a craps table, or sequentially hit a straight, a flush, and four of a kind on a video poker machine. I know that it's possible to gamble and win for hours, days, or even weeks at a time. It's also possible to lose consistently, regardless of skill and strategy. These volatile fluctuations are what make or break many casino gamblers, and every player should realize that these swings in fortune are a natural element of every casino game, and were predicted by the experts when long-term playing strategies were developed.

Another critical element that affects every player has to do with the application of correct (recommended) strategy during *actual* play. Once properly programmed, computers don't make mistakes, and since most of the experts' advice is based on computer-simulated play, there is essentially no chance of computer error. Unfortunately, the average gambler lacks the ability to play with machine-like precision, and strategy and wagering errors are commonplace. Mistakes occur because players misread cards, dice, or machine displays, make mathematical errors, place incorrect bets by confusing the denomination of their chips, or are otherwise distracted by physical playing conditions. These errors usually go unnoticed by the player because there is no guardian angel sitting on his shoulder, telling him the error of his ways!

I believe that most players, even those experienced and skilled at casino gambling, make mistakes in strategy and/or betting at least 3 percent of the time. Since most games and machines have long-term win/loss expectations of 1 percent to 6 percent, mistakes of this caliber seriously affect the outcome of play.

Two physiological factors also cause harm to otherwise expert players—effects of alcohol and fatigue. Free drinks and many hours of continuous exposure to the split-second demands of casino gambling cause serious wear and tear on our ability to function rationally. Again, without that guardian angel to oversee our actions, we often fail to realize that our playing decisions aren't meeting the guidelines recommended by the experts, and I can almost guarantee that the dealers and pit bosses aren't going to point out the error of our ways!

But on the other hand, I've seen drunk and bleary-eyed gamblers win tons of money within short periods of time! Another personal experience might help to explain this possibility. On my last trip to Las Vegas, I was staying at one of the downtown hotel/casinos, and began playing blackjack at 10:00 P.M. with intentions of playing for an hour or so and then retiring for the night. I lost *lots* of money in the first hour of play, and spent the next *fifteen* hours attempting to win back my losses! No serious money exchanged hands for a long lime. During the last hour of this extended playing session, I had several marvelous shoes, and gained back 90 percent of what I had lost in the first hour of play. Even though I didn't leave the table as a winner, I recovered most of my losses. Needless to say, I was exhausted after playing the longest session that I have ever experienced, and I don't recommend that you try this approach! In retrospect, I think I wagered about $60,000 during this extended playing session, and my total losses were less than $300!

So what's a person to do? The answer to this question is based on *how often* you plan to gamble. If you have $100 to risk, and your only goal is to double your money, *place one bet—make one wager—* on any of the games that offer one to one payoff. If you win this single bet, take your winnings and never enter a casino again.

If you are willing to accept a much greater chance of losing in hopes of winning much more than even odds, make your $100 bet on a single number on the roulette wheel, or a hard way bet on the craps table, or select ten numbers on a keno ticket, etc., etc. Play the long odds, quit whether you win or lose, and never gamble in a casino again.

Every expert that writes about casino gaming will tell you the informed player who plays *the least* has the best chance of making a profit! If you only make one wager in a game that has a house advantage of 3 percent on an even money bet, odds are that you will lose fifty-three times and win forty-seven times for every one hundred rounds played. The longer you play, the longer your bankroll is exposed to the built-in advantage held by the casino, so if you are going to bet in a casino, it's best to only make one wager, and then leave.

It's not likely that you are the type of gambler described above. I know I'm not! It's more likely that you plan to be in a casino for more time than it takes to place one bet. Since you purchased this book, it's probable that you enjoy gambling, hope to play for an extended period of time, and are reading this book in hopes of improving your chances of winning.

So we've come full circle. We know that the longer we play, the longer we expose ourselves to the casino's built-in advantage. We know that short-term play can be extremely volatile. We also know that following long-term strategy places arduous demands on our mental and physical capabilities and tests our faith in the accuracy and correctness of our playing and wagering decisions.

So why not ignore the tenets of long-term strategy, make decisions on the basis of inspiration and intuition, and rely on good luck to make you a winner? If you've spent any time in a casino, I'm sure that you have seen many players who gamble this way. Can you also play this way and come out ahead in the long run? In my opinion, and in the opinion of the experts, the answer is NO!

The experts base their advice once again on computer analysis. For instance, many blackjack players will not draw to a 16 when the dealer has a 7 or higher as his exposed card because they think they will bust the hand, and hope that the dealer instead will draw a bust card. The fact of the matter is that the experts have proven that this player hand is generally a loser, but that the player will *lose less in the long run* by hitting the 16. Similar analyses have been conducted for all sorts of decision-making situations in all types of casino gaming, and the experts' findings indisputably prove that the player who is in the game for the long run will be a long run loser if he fails to maximize his win potential by following the recommended strategies.

From a psychological standpoint, I'm much more comfortable playing according to the recommendations made by the experts. As a former schoolteacher, I believe in education and trust the opinions of informed teachers much more than I trust my instincts or intuition, and I quit relying on luck a long time ago!

I also find that it's much *easier* to play casino games if decisionmaking is predetermined and ingrained in my mind. Play becomes almost automatic, and allows me time to enjoy the entire casino experience without devoting all of my mental and emotional efforts to play-by-play decision making.

Simply stated, the smart casino gambler *must* follow the recommendations of established experts if he or she wishes to be a long-term potential winner. In spite of the weaknesses of the recommended strategies, they are still the best bet in the house. No matter how many hands you play, you only have two choices—either play *perfectly*, or play *poorly*. The *totality of your play* will be fairly close to the expert's projections, even if individual results of play deviate from the expected outcome.

Let Uncle Harry, and George, your best friend, and Mary, your husband's niece, be the ones to gamble by the seat of their pants, and you be the one who leaves the casino with a profit!

Money, Madness, Mathematics, and the Mental Edge

FRANK SCOBLETE

Mr. Scoblete is a player's writer. Unlike many of those who claim to be experts at casino gambling (but have spent very little time risking their money or testing their skills in actual casino play), Frank has been there, played the games, suffered his losses, relished his victories, and most important, learned from his experiences. This chapter tells you how to conquer your own emotions, as well as the casino.

Casino gambling is a twofold game. It is the physical or outer game that you are playing with its attendant rules, strategies, and money management systems. And it is the inner game that you are playing, where the principal opponent is not the other players, or the house edge, or the gods of chance, but one's own flawed self. To be a long-term winner, to even have a chance of winning, you must not only know the odds and the best systems and strategies to play, but you must also *know yourself.* Knowing yourself is an absolutely necessary ingredient for success. No matter how much you know about the games, no matter how astute you are with odds and analysis, if, in the heat of battle with casinos, your inner self becomes driven and crazed by the adrenaline rush of anticipation, success and/or disappointment, you are in BIG, BIG TROUBLE!

The ancients spoke of a "divine madness" or all-consuming frenzy that would give humans access to the gods and visionary powers to see the future. In gambling, the same thing can occur—only in reverse. The madness sets in, the frenzy becomes overpowering, and the future is easy to discern—for everyone, that is, but the player so enthralled. When the divine madness hits a casino gambler, his or her future is bleak.

To exemplify, let me tell you a story:

Before I ever placed a single serious bet in blackjack, I read two good books on the subject: Richard Canfield's *Blackjack Your Way to Riches* (Carol Publishing) and Ken Uston's *Two Books on Blackjack* (The Uston Institute of Blackjack). While Uston made a point of telling his readers that blackjack was a roller coaster ride with serious downs (not the least of which were casinos that barred skilled players from playing), I couldn't relate to his cautionary advice. It was Canfield's optimism and assurance that blackjack could be beaten *handily* that made the biggest impression on me at the time. I could become rich playing a simple card game in plush casinos! It doesn't get any better than that, I thought.

I learned basic strategy and card counting at home. I practiced endless hours. I even tried to duplicate the full-sensory experience that one encounters in a casino by blasting music while I practiced, and having my two sons attempt to distract me by practicing my game in their "playroom." ("Daddy, daddy, can Luke Skywalker defeat King Kong?" *High cards favor the player. Low cards favor the dealer.* "Dad, Greg just spit on my nose!" *Let's see…a six, five, king, three. Plus two!* "Mike, stay away from my action figures…Daaad! He's biting the head off Chewbacca!" *Two, ace five…now it's plus three.* "Daaad, the dog threw up the crayons all over the rug!")

When I felt that I could remember what I was doing amidst the din, I made up my mind to take on the casinos for real. I saved some money, and armed with Uston's strategies for Atlantic City blackjack, and buttressed by Canfield's enthusiastic recommendation of blackjack as my way to wealth, I set out for a week at the Tropicana (formerly Tropworld) with the beautiful A.P. (*Note: the beautiful A.P. is publisher and writer Alene Paone*).

Tropicana had a good four-deck game, and for seven days A.P. and I hammered them! Yes, it took me a few sessions to get used to playing in a casino but it wasn't all that hard. While there is a tremendous amount of noise, none of it was directed at me. I didn't hear, "Dad, can we go to the park?" or "Let's go to the movies—you promised!" as I had heard at home. I found it relatively easy to ignore the world around me and focus on what I was attempting to do, which was to become rich playing blackjack. And I knew I was going to become rich. We didn't have a losing session for a week—*not one!* I was giddy with success. It was so easy. We would sit down for a session—we played three sessions a day—and the casino basically handed us money! When the count got high, I'd get the blackjacks or 20s or, if I had a stiff the dealer would obligingly bust. Piece of cake. Canfield was right. Blackjack was an easy way to riches.

As A.P. and I walked along the boardwalk, I was making plans to move into a condo in Atlantic City.

"I figure we can buy it in a few months with our winnings," I said enthusiastically. "It shouldn't take too long. Then with the rest, we'll blah, blah, blah—" And I spun my fantasies. "Yes, Mr. Trump, I mean Donald, of course, *Don*, buddy, I'd be delighted to take part ownership in your casinos for the amount you owe me for my blackjack winnings. I hope you don't mind that Steve Wynn has also given me part ownership in his casinos because of all he owes me too."

A.P., always levelheaded, thought we should return to Atlantic City a few more times before uprooting ourselves. "After all, we might not always win," she cautioned.

"Nonsense," I said. "We have the edge." And I continued to dream all my dreams. At that time I was running a theater company in the New York area; I was producing, acting, and directing, but I was not at all happy with that life and the people I was dealing with. Blackjack looked like a safe and exciting way out. So, I dreamed my dreams, and three weeks later we returned to the Tropicana to win that down payment on the condo.

And we were destroyed!!

Destroyed, destroyed, destroyed!

I lost all the money I had won and all the money I had originally saved to play the game. Nothing went right. In high counts I lost my big bets. In low counts I'd win several in a row, with small bets up, then the count would rocket into the stratosphere, and I'd lose everything I had just won and then some. While I did have a few winning sessions, these were for paltry sums. They couldn't touch the amount I was losing in the other sessions.

And midway through the week I lost my head. I became literally mad. I was in a frenzy. Not only was I losing money, I was losing my dream. How could this be happening? I had the edge, damn it!

I started to sneak down in the wee hours of the morning before the casino closed (in those days, the Atlantic City casinos weren't open twenty-four hours a day) and before A.P. would wake up. Then I'd be the first down in the morning to play.

As for A.P., she had been immobilized. She had stopped playing all but a few sessions with me. She was in a state of shock, and she recommended that we leave Atlantic City, go home, and regroup.

I didn't want to regroup! I wanted to recoup my losses, so I started betting more. In high counts, I'd put up huge bets in the hope that I could win a few bets and make back all that I had lost. I had the edge, damn it! I had the edge! I stopped taking walks, I stopped going to the spa. All I wanted to do was play and play and play some more.

By the sixth day, we were broke—largely thanks to me. Every penny that we had brought with us to gamble with was gone. Every penny we had originally saved to gamble with was gone. I didn't even have the presence of mind to think to myself, "Thank God, you are only playing with extra money, not money that you need for bills and kids and all of the other essentials of life." I couldn't think that way at all. The money I had lost, while technically *extra*, was still *money* and thus as real, tangible, and palpable as money reserved for life's necessities.

So we left the city, totally defeated.

On the way back to New York, we decided to drop in on the Captain (see my books *Beat the Craps out of the Casinos: How to Play Craps and Win!* and *The Captain's Craps Revolution!*) I had just become aware of this remarkable man's craps systems and, more importantly, I needed someone with experience to talk to.

We rang the bell and the Captain himself answered. He looked at me. He looked at A.P. and he said knowingly, "Here they are with empty pockets."

How did he know?

"There's a big sign written on your forehead," he said to me "It says, 'I have lost everything, including my dignity.' "

I hadn't exactly thought of it that way, but he was right. Losing that much cash was traumatic, but what really necessitated my visit to the Captain was not the substantial monetary loss, but the fact that I had lost my head. Unlike the heroes of Ernest Hemingway's novels, I had displayed anything but grace under fire. The Captain knew this. He could read it in my face.

"How did I know?" he repeated as we sat in his study. "Because I've been there. Every serious player at one time or another faces the abyss when he plays. That abyss is usually a series of losses that are then compounded by a loss of composure, leading to a devastating loss or a devastating series of losses. The casino player is a tightrope walker. Once he loses his balance, it's a long plunge to the ground."

The Captain then explained some of his ideas. A person who experiences what the beautiful A.P. and I had been through will do one of several things. Having lost his balance, he stays that way—unbalanced. He becomes a foolish gambler, risking money wildly, often on bad bets that pay back long odds, in a continuous effort to instantly win back all of his previous losses. This type of person will also try to push small wins into big wins and big wins into gigantic wins and gigantic wins into titanic wins until ultimately he loses some, most, or everything that he had won and then some. People who dive in for the titanic win end up at the bottom of the gambling sea. Or, a person having confronted the abyss, gives up his desire to play or is scared away by thoughts of experiencing such devastation in the future. Or, he can learn from such epic defeats and come back a stronger, wiser, better player.

"It wasn't the fact that you lost," said the Captain. "You are going to lose. You are going to have losing streaks. Even when you have the edge, as a card counter does in blackjack, you will have bad days, or weeks, or even months. That is to be expected. But like a fighter, you have to go into your fight with a game plan. You have to fight your fight, not the casino's fight. You have to set the pace. The casino's pace is go, go, go, play all day, play all night. The casino is geared to making otherwise sane people insane when they play. They want you to lose your head because then you'll lose your money. The player, on the other hand, has to have a slower rhythm. You have to set your pace and you have to have a deliberate pace. Play a session with a predetermined goal in mind. Usually it's a loss limit mixed with some money management principles that will allow you to capitalize on winning streaks when they occur."

"And always be prepared to leave if things are going badly. One of your mistakes was to change the time of your sessions due to hysteria, not calculation. There was no point in playing extra sessions that only fatigued you and probably led to mistakes in play. Instead, you should have scheduled an extra walk on the boardwalk or an extra swim in the pool or an extra nap. You should have cut down your playing time, lowered your bets, and stretched your money so that it would last the entire week. You were on the psychological ropes and despite the fact that you had an edge, you couldn't make the money back. You should have tried to last, not knock the casino out with big bets. Deep down even as you were doing that, you were aware of the fact that you were fighting a stupid fight against a strong opponent, and he was winning due not only to his superior strength but to your stupidity. That's what hurt the most."

The Captain was right, of course. I had played like a complete and utter fool, and subconsciously I had been aware of that. A.P. had not fared much better but at least she knew enough to want to end our trip early and go home to regroup. But I had persisted in my folly, much as Agamemnon did when he refused to listen to reason and instead offered his daughter as a sacrifice in order to fight the Trojan War, a war fought to recover a faithless wife. As the Greek playwright Aeschylus said, "The greatest gift from the gods is a mind free from folly."

That Tropicana experience was my madness and my folly. That was many, many years ago, and since then I've had many winning sessions. I've also had losing sessions. Indeed, I've had some bad (meaning big) losing sessions—even some bad losing weeks! I've gone to my room on more than one occasion, curled up on the bed in a fetal position, and asked myself why I do this. Why do I challenge the Fates?

Then I take a nap, or go for a walk or a swim. Oh yes, I am now prepared for the fact that I will lose on occasion (don't get me wrong—I still *hate* losing), but I no longer lose my cool when I lose my money. I fight my fight—win, lose or draw. I know that if the casino is going to beat me, it is going to beat me without my help because I will never again beat myself.

And on the flip side, on many occasions I have stood on the

Strip, looked at all the thousands of people hurrying and scurrying, and I know what few others have known. I know what it is like to defeat the mighty casinos at their own games!

However, while total self-control is a necessary condition for winning, it is not the *only* necessary condition. You can have total control, be as cool as cool can be, but if you play games that a high house edge *you are most likely to kiss your money goodbye*. There is no way to come home a consistent winner if you are putting your money into games that give the casino a giant edge.

And what is a "giant" edge? Many authors and experts disagree on this aspect of casino gambling. Purists will say that *any* game with *any* house is a bad game. For them the only games worth considering are games where expert play can give the player the edge. These games include (but aren't limited to) card counting in specific blackjack games, expert play on some video poker machines, regular poker, Pai Gow poker (bank only), roulette (biased wheel play) and expert sports betting. The list is not long, and even the most skilled players can't beat all the games offered in most casinos. Unfortunately, the most skilled players (especially in blackjack) run the risk of being banned or otherwise thwarted from playing the beatable games once the casinos recognize their expertise.

The nonpurists run the gamut from authors and "experts" who have a mistaken notion of what constitutes having the odds in one's favor to those individuals who don't care about the odds and offer oddball advice based on idiosyncratic assumption.

I'm somewhat in between these two extremes. I recognize that to win in the long run, you must have the mental and mathematical edge—these are the M & M's of gambling. However, I recognize that some games are not to the liking of all people. There are many people who prefer machines to table games. Many table game players don't want to apply the concentration required to become an expert blackjack card counter. People play for different reasons:

- some play just for the money;
- some play for the money, the pleasure, and the challenge;
- some play for the pleasure and the challenge, and *then* for the money;
- some play only for the pleasure; forget the challenge or the money.

I fit the second category. I play for the money, the pleasure, and the challenge. With the exception of the last category (What pleasure can there be if you don't have at least a decent shot at winning some money? Pick a game that doesn't cost anything to play!) all the reasons that people would gamble in a casino are equally valid. As long as the notion that winning some money is a reason for being in a casino, then as a nonpurist I can recommend and approach to games that will satisfy the conditions of challenge, pleasure, and, perhaps, profit.

My guess is that anyone reading this book has a desire to become a good player—why else bother to purchase and read it? You can be a rotten player just by going to a casino and betting up a storm.

In addition, my experience indicates that people who read books on casino gambling intend to go more than once or twice a year to casinos and are looking for ways to reduce their losses, increase their chances of winning, and extend the pleasurable time they spend in the casinos. Not everyone is looking for a mathematical edge, but everyone should be looking to reduce the house edge to manageable proportions.

What are manageable proportions? I have a rather arbitrary idea of what constitutes an acceptable house edge. I think that any house edge that is *over 1.5 percent* is too much for the player to overcome. However, a house edge of 1.5 percent or lower allows you to have a decent chance of winning, especially if you're only playing for a day or a few days several times a year.

An Overview of Casino Gambling—Then and Now

JOHN GROCHOWSKI

John Grochowski's columns on casino gaming appear twice a week in the Chicago Sun-Times, and one column is syndicated to other newspapers through the Sun-Times Features syndicate. He has written two excellent books on gaming, *Winning Tips for Casino Games,* and *Gaming: Cruising the Casinos With Syndicated Gambling Columnist John Grochowski.* (Incidentally, his name is pronounced Jon Grow-how-ski).

John has been a speaker at many gaming expos and symposiums, and hosts television segments on casino gaming twice a week on "Chicago Racing Report" on SportsChannel Chicago. He is a frequent contributor to a number of magazines, including Casino Executive, International Gaming and Wagering Business, and Midwest Gaming and Travel.

John has spent much of his twenty-two-year newspaper career as a sportswriter, and has recently earned the title of "Mr. Midwest Gaming," unofficially awarded to him by other writers of casino gambling literature. For information on John's latest book, *Gaming,* a 182-page collection of sixty-five of his columns, plus two gaming-oriented travel features, call Huntington Press.

As I'm typing this chapter in my home office in the Chicago suburbs, I'm just a forty-five-minute drive from eleven casinos. I can hop in my car and head west to seven riverboat casinos in Illinois, or head east to four Indiana Lake Michigan cruisers.

I could take a little longer drive west and within a couple of hours check out riverboats in Illinois and Iowa, as well as slot machines at Iowa racetracks. A few hours more and I could test my luck at riverboats in other parts of Illinois and Missouri, or could wander north to land-based Native American casinos in Wisconsin.

These opportunities don't exist because I happen to live in the Midwestern crossroads that is Chicago. Nearby casino gaming options are common for the majority of Americans as we close in on the twenty-first century. Steve Bourie's 1997 *American Casino Guide* lists nearly six hundred in thirty states. From the card rooms of California to the charity casinos of Maryland, from the barges of Mississippi to the Native American facilities in Minnesota, casinos have become so much a part of life in the lower forty-eight states that the outpost is remote indeed if it's not within a few hours of a place to play.

It's been less than a decade since legalized casino gambling began to break out of its traditional homes in Nevada and New Jersey. The federal government didn't authorize gaming on Native American lands until 1988, and it was three years later that Iowa became the first state to launch a riverboat casino.

In that scant time, casinos have become part of the entertainment mainstream in the United States. Harrah's annual survey released in 1996 concludes that in 1995, Americans made 154 million casino visits—11 million more than attendance at amusement parks, and only slightly less than the 177 million who attended games offered by Major League Baseball, the National Football League, the National Basketball Association, the National Hockey League, NCAA Division 1 football and basketball, and the PGA and Senior golf tours!

This would never have been possible in the days when going to a casino meant hopping a plane for Las Vegas or Reno.

Where we play has changed, and what we play has changed. If we were to take a time machine back, say, four decades, we'd hardly recognize what we would see.

1958:—Let's jump in our time machine, turn back the clock, and visit a casino in 1958. We try to explain to a sympathetic pit boss what ifs like in our world—where most Americans have easy access to casinos, where blackjack is far and away the most-played table game but with a popularity that is dwarfed by slot machines, where the boys dealing craps are as likely as not to be girls. As his eyes glaze over, the pit boss tells us, "Sure, pal. Why don't you call it a night and sleep it off?"

Blackjack? Sure, there's blackjack on the casino floor in 1958. Simple game. One deck of fifty-two cards, see who gets closer to 21 without busting, you or the dealer. Maybe the first card off the deck is buried, but the players get to see it. And if the dealer runs out of cards in the middle of a hand, he shuffles the remainder and continues dealing. It's regarded as a sucker's game, though. The real gambling is done at the craps tables!

Craps is the most popular casino game of the day, and no wonder. Look at who the players are. They're all men, and an awful lot of them served in World War II. Some of the younger players fought in Korea, and they share a link—the barracks and the foxholes where they learned to shoot craps. The serviceman's game of the wartime generation fuels the casino trade of the fifties.

Women or kids? Maybe the women to blow on the dice for luck, but rarely as a player and never as a dealer. Sure, the casino hires women. There's a cocktail waitress now. There are a few wives and girlfriends around, but the kids aren't welcome, wanted, or allowed. The slot machines are for the women. The one-armed bandits keep the ladies entertained while their men do the serious gambling. If the man rolls high enough, the house will even see that his wife is taken care of with rolls of nickels for the slots.

Nickels. That's the coin of the realm when it comes to slots. There are penny machines, and some quarters, but slots are a five-cent game. One nickel at a time and maybe, if the player is lucky, she'll hit a winner and have twenty or thirty nickels come pouring out. The coin tubes that drop winnings into the player's tray can't hold more than that. A really big jackpot, *one hundred nickels,* has to be paid by hand.

Oh, there are other games. The sports book is an important part of the casino. The roulette wheel is always busy. The Sands just added some European game. Chemin de fer, they call it. And the Stardust is just about to add something similar called baccarat. Video poker? You want poker, try the card room. There's no "video" though. There's Keno, Hazard, Bingo, and some old carnival games like Chuck-A-Luck and the Big-Six wheel.

The Sands and the Stardust are new and beautiful in 1958. The Las Vegas Strip has come a long way since Bugsy Siegel opened the fabulous Flamingo in 1947. It didn't work out for Bugsy—when he lost money in the first couple of weeks the boys had to take over the business and he suffered an untimely death—but look at it now! The Thunderbird in 1948, Desert Inn in 1950, Sahara and Sands in 1952, Riviera and Dunes in 1955, Hacienda in 1956, Tropicana in 1957, and Stardust in 1958. The Strip is the center of the gambling universe. If you don't play here you can go downtown or up to Reno, or try your luck at the casinos operating outside the law in New Orleans, Miami, or Cleveland. But time flies, so we choose to move on...

1978:—Back to the time machine we go, and leap ahead twenty years. Now it's 1978, the year of the great breakout. Casino gaming is no longer confined to Nevada!

Resorts International has become the first casino to open in Atlantic City, basically with the same games offered in Nevada but without a sports book (which is illegal in New Jersey). There's fear in Las Vegas, we're told, that with casinos practically in their backyard the New York and Philadelphia crowd won't go west anymore. Are the Nevada boom days over?

At a cursory glance the games look the same as in 1958—but what's happened to the game of blackjack? All the players' cards are being dealt faceup, and the dealer's sliding them out of a box instead of pitching them from the top of a deck. How many decks does that shoe hold? Four? Six?

What happened was a *revolution*, one that was just beginning back in 1958. The publication of Edward O. Thorp's *Beat the Dealer* in 1962 let the public in on the secret that blackjack is a beatable game for card counters. Never mind that most bettors will not learn how to count cards, and even those who do won't do it well enough to cause the casinos any real trouble. The idea that a casino game was actually beatable caught the public's imagination.

By the time we arrive in 1978, nearly half of all gaming tables are devoted to blackjack. It has long surpassed craps as the most popular table game, and is now the casinos' biggest moneymaker.

The Blackjack Revolution neither begins nor ends with Thorp. In 1956, the first basic strategy was published by four U.S. Army mathematicians (led by Roger Baldwin) in the *Journal of the American Statistical Association*. Julian Braun of IBM in Chicago followed with the first computer study of the game, which would smooth out the rough edges in basic strategy and turn single-deck games, as played in the fifties, into an even game. Serious blackjack analysis starts here—from Thorp to Lawrence Revere's *Playing Blackjack as a Business* to Ken Uston's development of team play that he'll write about in *Million Dollar Blackjack* (written in 1981) to later works by Peter Griffin (*The Theory of Blackjack*), Arnold Snyder (*Blackbelt in Blackjack*), Stanford Wong (*Basic Blackjack* and *Professional Blackjack*) and more.

As *Beat the Dealer* became a bestseller, it raised a panic in the casino industry. Dealers started shuffling up before reaching the end of the deck and clamped down on the rules, forbidding players the splitting of Aces and restricting doubling-downs to totals of 11. The tight rules had the opposite effect of that desired by the casinos, because the good players still won but the average players stayed away from the tables. Casinos quickly restored the old rules and looked for other countermeasures.

By the time we arrive in 1978, casinos have adopted as their primary countermeasure the use of multiple-deck shoes, with as many as eight decks in play at one time. Players no longer see all the cards; the dealer might shuffle up with as many as half the cards remaining in the shoe. There are still some single-deck games, but dealers shuffle long before reaching the end of the deck.

At the same time as the blackjack revolution, another enormous change is hitting the casinos—the slot machine revolution, which began in the mid-sixties when Bally's introduced the "Money Honey?" slot. It was a traditional three-reel, handle-on-the-side machine, but it had something that earlier slots didn't have—a hopper to circulate coins. That made it possible for the machine to spit out more than twenty or thirty coins at a time, unlike the fifties slots, and made it possible to offer multiple-coin, multiple-payline machines.

Also, the mechanical innards of slot machines are being replaced by electronics, using solid-state technology. Now there are ringing bells and flashing lights, attracting attention to slots. Electronics also makes possible the first progressive jackpots. Dollar machines are making inroads, and casinos are offering higher payout percentages than ever before.

Slots are starting to catch up to table games in popularity. In the late seventies they produced about 30 percent of revenue in Las Vegas casinos. Men are joining women at the slots, and women are starting to join men at the tables—and behind the tables, too. Due to the new equal employment opportunities requirements and the opening of hundreds of jobs in Atlantic City, women are starting to take jobs in the casinos that would not have been open to them twenty years earlier.

Due to the expansion of both blackjack and slots, other games have had their floor space cut back. Craps is still a favorite of the wartime generation and the second most popular table game, but younger players prefer the "beatable" blackjack. The carnival games are declining in number, though nearly everyone still has a Big Six or money wheel. No casino is complete without roulette, though it too is in decline. Sic Bo and Pai-Gow have carved out places in casinos that attract travelers from Asia.

Baccarat, which when we last checked was about to make its Las Vegas debut, has become big business. It's now a favorite of the high rollers, played in roped-off areas or separate rooms reserved for those with big bankrolls. The action of a few big bettors, win or lose, shows up in the bottom lines of the houses that cater to high-stakes baccarat players.

Where do we play? Atlantic City has been added to Las Vegas and Reno as a prime gaming destination. Soon there will be a dozen casinos in Atlantic City. On the Vegas Strip, Caesars Palace, opened in 1966, has started a trend toward luxurious megaresorts, and Circus Circus, opened in 1968, makes the first bid to attract a clientele other than hard-core gamblers. Casino gambling is on the upswing, and it's time for us to return to the present.

1998—Gaming today: As we return home to the late 1990s, the changes are even greater than those that separated 1978 from 1958. The fears that the availability of gaming in Atlantic City would gut Las Vegas proved to be unfounded. In fact, in the face of nationwide gaming, Las Vegas is having its biggest growth spurt and was the fastest-growing city in the United States three years in a row. In 1995, gaming revenues in Las Vegas accounted for $5.2 billion of Nevada's total $7 billion, compared with $3.7 billion in Atlantic City. The rest of the nation realized $9.6 billion in casino revenues, with $4.5 billion of that coming from Native American operations in twenty states. Mississippi ($1.7 billion), Illinois ($1.2 billion), and

Louisiana ($1.1 billion) all joined Nevada and New Jersey in cracking the billion-dollar annual revenue mark.

Today we have players, dealers, even supervisors who have never set foot in either Nevada or New Jersey. The trend toward bigger, themed megaresorts that began in the sixties continues across the country, complete with recreational and care facilities for youngsters and teenagers. Las Vegas remains the center of the gambling universe. The Mirage with its volcano, the MGM Grand with its enormous lion face, the pirate ships of Treasure Island, the pyramid and Sphinx Luxor, and the skyline of New York, New York, are but a few of the recent additions to the Las Vegas Strip.

But now Missouri has its Kansas City Station with a 140,000-square-foot casino that dwarfs the Strip resorts of the fifties and sixties. Connecticut has its Foxwoods with 139,000 square feet of gaming space in one of the world's busiest casinos. Minnesota and Mississippi have huge Grand Casinos, the proving ground for the company that now runs Las Vegas' Stratosphere Tower, the tallest building west of the Mississippi.

With all the new customers attracted by the expansion of gambling has come new ways to play. Foremost is the continued expansion of slot machines. Modern machines are controlled by microprocessors programmed with random number generators that determine what combinations will show on the reels. Computer technology has made possible huge progressive jackpots, exceeding $10 million on dollar machines.

Slot manufacturers also can put several games on one machine, allowing the customer to switch back and forth between games at a touch of a button, or a touch of a screen. The revolution continues with the beginning of a switch away from chip-based micro-processors to slot machines with hard drives. By the end of 1996, Bally's Las Vegas was giving a floor test to a new machine from Silicon Gaming programmed with a stunning array of video and special effects, mirroring the computer revolution in everyday life.

Customers have responded to nineties slots in a big way. More than 70 percent of casino revenue comes from electronic gaming devices—that's video poker, video blackjack, video keno and other specialty games, as well as reel slots.

Those nickel machines that ruled the slots when we started our journey in 1958 have been pushed into the background. Many casinos offer no nickel slots at all. The quarter and dollar machines are the most-played games in the house, and there are now $5, $25, even $100 slot machines.

The dollar slot player is king. Newer machines are fitted with bill validators and credit meters that allow a customer to play without dropping in coins for every handle pull. That enables the dollar slot player to play so fast he's as valuable to the casino as a $50 table player. That shows in the spread of slot clubs—player tracking systems that allow the casino to reward slot players with the kind of room and meal comps that had always been reserved for those serious gamblers at the tables. Steve Wynn introduced the slot club at the Golden Nugget in Atlantic City in 1982, then brought it to Las Vegas in 1984. Today it's a rare casino that doesn't have a player tracking system on the slots.

Next to slot machines, what's the most popular game? One that some people lump in with slots, actually. Video poker, unheard of in 1958 and still under development in the labs of Fortune Coin Company in Las Vegas and A-1 Supply Company in Reno in 1978, now accounts for one-quarter of all shipments of electronic gaming devices. The more people play video poker, the more popular it gets. In newer gaming destinations, video poker accounts for only 5 to 10 percent of games on the slot floor. But try walking into a locals-oriented casino in Las Vegas sometime—the Gold Coast or the Fiesta, for example. Half or more of the gaming space is taken up by video poker.

At the tables, blackjack remains the most popular game. Players still think it's beatable, and most players still can't beat it. Roughly half of all table game revenues come from blackjack.

But per casino, table game space is shrinking as slots expand. Table game managers have responded with a flow of new games and gimmicks added to old games. There's been an attempt to bring baccarat to the masses with mini-baccarat—same rules, but faster-paced play because the player doesn't handle the cards. Red Dog, a variation on Acey-Deucey, made its way to some casino floors. Pai-Gow poker, a slow-paced version of Pai Gow that uses playing cards instead of Asian tiles, has carved out a niche. Spanish 21, a version of blackjack in which the rules are liberalized but 10-spots are removed from the deck, has started to catch on. Three Card poker, in which a player can win either by beating the dealer or by catching certain hands, achieved some popularity in Mississippi in 1996. A few casinos are even trying Casino War, basically the child's game of war.

But the unquestioned kings of the new games are Caribbean Stud poker and Let It Ride. Both are based on five-card stud poker and have joined the list of standard casino games that are offered nearly everywhere. Caribbean Stud is even pushing roulette as the third most popular table game, behind blackjack and craps.

Interestingly, one popular gaming option that never spread was the sports book. Legal, full-scale sports gambling is confined to Nevada. A federal law passed in the early nineties made it illegal for states that didn't already have it to add sports betting.

Not only has *where* we play changed, and *what* we play changed, but who plays has also changed. Remember how back in 1958, the casino attracted men to the tables and a handful of women to the slots? Today men and women play in equal proportions, and casino population reflects the U. S. population as a whole. The Harrah's survey mentioned earlier found that of casino customers in 1995, 50 percent were men, 50 percent women; they had a median household income of $39,000 (U.S. average $31,000), a median age of 47 (U.S.

average 46), and 50 percent had at least some college education (U.S. overall 49 percent).

The changes that occur in casinos aren't designed to attract some specialized clientele. They're designed to attract you and me and the woman next door and the guy down the street. If we want to play more slots, there'll be more slots; if we want to play Caribbean Stud, there'll be Caribbean Stud.

We probably can even look forward to the development of regional games. Gaming outside Nevada and New Jersey is so new that the starting point at nearly every operation is a mix of games that have worked in traditional gaming destinations. But who's to say that Mississippi won't develop into the Three Card poker capital of the world, or that Coloradoans won't go crazy for Spanish 21 or that Minnesota won't take to heart some game that we don't even know yet?

There's an exciting new world of gaming out there, one that will make 2018 as different from 1998 as 1978 was from 1958. And we're just at the beginning.

GLOSSARY OF BLACKJACK TERMINOLOGY

Action   The amount wagered over a period of time.

Anchor   The last player to the dealer's right at a blackjack table.

Back counting   A card counting technique wherein the player does not enter the game until the count is in his favor.

Bank   Whoever covers all bets (usually the casino).

Bankroll   The total amount that the player has to spend on a session of play.

Basic strategy   A playing system that provides the long-run, optimal way to play, based on the player's cards and the dealer's exposed card.

Bet   The player's wager on each hand of play.

Blackjack   The most common name for the game of 21.

Blacks   Casino chips valued at $100 each.

Break   When the player or dealer exceed a point count of twenty-one points.

Burn card   The first card discarded from the deck or shoe.

Bust   Same as break.

Buy-in   The amount of cash exchanged for chips at the initiation of play.

Cage   The cashier's section of a casino.

Casino host   A casino employee who caters to big bettors.

Casino manager   The chief casino executive on duty.

Chip   The monetary token used in lieu of cash.

Counter   A player who applies a card counting system.

Comp   Complimentary lodging, food, services, or gifts provided by the casino to qualified players.

Cut card   A solid colored card, usually plastic, used to cut the deck.

Dealer   The person who deals the game.

Double-down   A playing rule which allows the player to double his original bet and be dealt one, and only one, card to his hand.

First base   The first player on the dealer's left at the start of each hand.

Flat bet   A bet of the same monetary amount on each hand; the amount wagered never varies.

Flash   To see the dealer's unexposed card.

Front money   Cash required and deposited with the casino in order to receive comps.

Grifter   A gambler who cheats.

Grinder   A small money bettor.

Hard hand   A hand without an ace, or a hand where the ace can only be counted as one point.

High roller   A gambler who plays for high stakes.

Hit   A single card received by a player or dealer.

Hole card   The unexposed card in a hand.

Hot   A player or dealer on a winning streak.

House   The gambling establishment; the casino.

Junket   A short gambling trip whose travel costs are usually paid for by the casino.

Marker   A casino document which allows a player to draw chips against his credit or cash on deposit.

Match play chips or coupons   A comp given to a player which allows him to match the amount of the chip with a like amount of cash on a single wager, and receive the amount of the cash wager and the match play chip if he wins the hand.

Mechanic   A person (usually a dealer) who is proficient at cheating.

Odds   The probability of winning a hand.

Pat hand   A hand to which no further cards need be drawn.

Perks   Minor comps received by a player.

Pit boss   A supervisor of one or more blackjack tables.

Point count   The total number of points in a player's hand. Also, a card counter's summation.

Push   A tie hand between the dealer and the player.

Press   To increase a wager after winning a hand (usually double the original wager).

Rich deck   A partial deck that has a disproportionately high percentage of face cards and aces.

Running count   The count maintained in card counting systems as each card is dealt.

Session   The amount of time devoted to play without leaving the table.

Shill   A casino employee who poses as a player in order to attract other players into a game.

Shoe   The container from which multiple-deck games are dealt.

Soft hand   A hand with an ace which is counted as eleven points.

Stand   The decision to receive no further cards.

Stiff   A hand with a hard point count of twelve to sixteen points.

Strategy   A method of play based on long-term probabilities.

Surrender   A casino rule which allows a player to discontinue play after receiving the first two cards by losing half of the amount wagered.

System   Same as strategy.

Table games   Casino games where the players sit or stand around a table.

Tactic   A short-term system or strategy.

Third base   Same as anchor.

Toke   A tip, or a wager placed for the dealer.

Unit   The dollar amount of a basic bet; one chip.

Walk away a winner   The object of playing blackjack!

BIBLIOGRAPHY

(AND SUGGESTED READING)

Bourie, Steve. *1995 Casino/Resort, Riverboat, and FunBook Guide*. Dania, FL: Casino Vacations, 1994.

Bourie, Steve. *1997 American Casino Guide*. Dania, FL: Casino Vacations, 1995.

Cardoza, Avery. *Winner's Playbook*. New York: Cardoza Publishing, 1995.

Casino Player—The Magazine for Gaming Enthusiasts. West Atlantic City, NJ: Ace Marketing, Inc., 1995.

Curtis, Anthony. *Bargain City—Booking, Betting, and Beating the New Las Vegas*. Huntington Press, 1993.

Dahl, Donald. *Progression Blackjack*. New York: Carol Publishing Group Edition, 1995.

Edwards, Mary Jane and Greg. *Bet On It—The Ultimate Guide to Nevada*. Memphis, TN: Mustang Publishing Co., 1992.

Humble, Lance and Carl Cooper. *The World's Greatest Blackjack Book*, New York: Doubleday, 1987.

Martin, Don and Betty Woo. *The Best of Nevada*. Columbia, CA: Pine Cone Press, 1992.

Ortiz, Darwin. *Darwin Ortiz on Casino Gambling*. New York: Carol Publishing Group Edition, 1995.

Outcalt, J. K. *Nationwide Directory of Licensed Gambling Establishments*. Gainesville, FL: Outcalt and Associates, Inc., 1994.

Patrick, John. *John Patrick's Blackjack*. New York: Carol Publishing Group Edition, 1995.

Patterson, Jerry L. *Blackjack—A Winner's Handbook*. New York: Perigee Books, 1990.

Revere, Lawrence. *Playing Blackjack as a Business*. New York: Carol Publishing Group Edition, 1994.

Roberts, Stanley. *The Gambling Times Guide to Blackjack*. New York: Carol Publishing Group Edition, 1994.

Silberstang, Edwin. *The Winner's Guide to Casino Gambling*. New York: Signet, 1003.

Scarne, John. *Scarne's New Complete Guide to Gambling*. New York: Simon and Schuster, 1986.

Scoblete, Frank. *Guerrilla Gambling*. Bonus Books, Inc., 1993.

Tamburin, Henry J. *The Ten Best Casino Bets*. 2d ed. Mobile, AL: Research Services Unlimited, 1994.

Thomason, Walter and Cynthia. *A Family Guide to Gambling in the U.S.A.—A National Directory for "Players" and Their Families*. 1994–1995 ed. Ft. Lauderdale, FL: 1994.

Thomason, Walter. *Blackjack—35 Tips to Make You a Winner!! A Basic Guide for the Game of "21"*. Ft. Lauderdale, FL: 1995.

Thompson, William N. *Legalized Gambling—A Reference Handbook*. Santa Barbara, CA: ABC-CLIO, Inc., 1994.

Thorp, Edward O. *Beat the Dealer: A Winning Strategy for the Game of Twenty One*. New York: Blaisdell Publishing Co., 1962.

Uston, Ken. *Million Dollar Blackjack*. Hollywood, CA: SRS Enterprises, 1981.

ADDITIONAL RESOURCES

Current and up-to-the-minute information about blackjack is contained in the magazines and periodicals listed below, along with publication schedules and subscription telephone numbers or addresses:

Blackjack Confidential Magazine (Eight issues annually) P.O. Box 8087, Cherry Hill, NJ 08002-0087.
Blackjack Forum (Quarterly) 1-510-465-6452.
Casino Journal's National Gaming Summary (Weekly) Fax 1-702-253-6805.
Casino Player Magazine (Monthly) 1-800-969-0711.
Las Vegas Advisor (Monthly newsletter and book sales) 1-800-244-2224.
Las Vegas Insider (Monthly newsletter and book sales) 602-636-1649.

Two bookstores that specialize in gambling-related publications, and are pleased to send you a free catalog, are listed below.

Gambler's Book Club, 1-800-522-1777.

The Gambler's Edge, 4344 S. Archer Ave., Chicago, IL 60632.